For Ruth and Dick Hale

ONE CHURCH
MANY CONGREGATIONS

Thomas Weber

Tom Weber

Fairway Press, Lima, Ohio

ONE CHURCH MANY CONGREGATIONS

FIRST EDITION
Copyright © 2001 by
Thomas Weber

Library of Congress Catalog Card Number: 2001 131705

ISBN 0-7880-1689-X

PRINTED IN U.S.A.

I Corinthians 12:4-7

Now there are varieties of gifts but the same spirit, and there are varieties of service, but the same God; and there are varieties of working, but it is the same God who inspires them in everyone. To each is given the manifestation of the Spirit for the common good.

The Brief Statement of Faith, 1991.

In gratitude of God, empowered by the Spirit, we strive to serve Christ in our daily tasks, and to live holy and joyful lives.

Table of Contents

About the author: Thomas Weber is an elder of the church and associate professor of history at Douglass College. He retired in 1978.

PREFACE

The sources for this study include the church's Annual Reports, the monthly Parish News, and weekly Sunday bulletins over many years. I subscribe to and read the Presbyterian Outlook, a weekly publication serving the Presbyterian Church, and I do more general reading on the social and political history of the nation in the last half century. I have also drawn on several talks given in the Adult Education Forum on particular topics in the recent history of the congregation. In the church I served as Clerk of Session from 1983 to 1989, and during several years in the 1990s I was trained for and served as a Stephen Minister. I have participated over a long period of time in several different music activities, and in various programs in Christian Education. For a time I helped the Mission Committee with preparation and delivery of a monthly meal to the homeless families at the Ozanam Shelter. In all these activities, and others, I have gotten to know many wonderful people in the congregation, most considerably younger. I have noticed their ways of participating in church activities and their attitudes about why this is important in their lives, all of which has greatly strengthened my own faith. Out of love for this congregation, I wrote this story to say thank you for your inspiration. The book also incorporates material originally written for the observance of the church's 250th anniversary in 1967.

October 10, 2000

Thomas Weber
Edison, New Jersey

Chapter I

THE FOUR CONGREGATIONS AND
THEIR PATTERN OF CHANGE

The earlier volume on the history of our church, written during the 1960s, was a historical account from its earliest presence in the Metuchen area in 1717 to the completion of its last major building program in 1958. The two dates are inscribed on the cornerstone of the church. The book was organized around the ministers who served the congregation across the years. The present account fulfills two different goals. One is to complete the history of our congregation in the last forty years, including the difficult years of the sixties and seventies, and the rebuilding of the church community in the eighties and nineties. The other goal is to review our history in terms of the various congregations that have been the heart of our existence, beginning in 1787 when our first congregation began its career independent from its mother church in Woodbridge. In other words, this book is not about our pastors; it's about us.

The structure of the Presbyterian Church in America, consisting of Presbyteries, Synods, and General Assembly, was built in the eighteenth century on the foundation of its congregations. Our mother church was originally founded as a Puritan Congregational Church. The Presbytery of Philadelphia was established in 1706 to protect the interests of the ministers, who were under threat of persecution by the Anglican Church as the official church of the royal colony of New Jersey. The Woodbridge Church and others joined the Presbytery. In time more Presbyteries, then a Synod were organized, and in 1789 the General Assembly was created. The General Assembly is a delegate body, which meets annually, with equal representation of lay members and clergy; its composition changes each time it meets. It elects a Moderator for a one-year term. Each year there is a new Moderator, making an ever-changing national leadership. Presbyteries act as a resource and support to the congregations in their area, and provide standards for the employment of clergy.

One of the consequences of this structure is that it leaves major authority in the hands of the congregation, the community of the faithful and the foundation of the church. The congregation elects its own governing body and approves the terms of call of its pastors, who are members of Presbytery. It develops the programs, services and ministries that seem best to carry out its mission, under the guidance of its clergy. As that mission changes, affected by external events and by changes in the congregation, different congregations develop to meet new challenges. In the Presbyterian structure, it is also true that the success of a congregation's endeavors depends on a strong and positive link with its pastor. Though there are different styles of pastoral leadership, the weakening or severance of that bond can easily cause a congregation to lose its confidence and begin to drift aimlessly.

Over the more than 200 years since 1787, the people who carried out the responsibilities of the congregation have done so in different ways, with different characteristics, and with varying degrees of success. For instance, we began with seventy members, hovered between 200 and 300 in the nineteenth and early twentieth centuries, and only in our most recent fifty years has church membership exceeded 1,000. For the first seventy years of our existence we were known as the Second Presbyterian Church of Woodbridge, the only church in the area, and our original home was a small meeting house located in the old colonial cemetery.

But the distinctions go much deeper than simply names and numbers. Over our long history, it is possible to distinguish four separate congregations, to which we can attach identifying labels. The first congregation, the Village Church, organized in 1787, created the basic services in worship and began a Sunday school, increasing its membership to become a permanent presence in the community. In time, willing to take a risk to fulfill a vision of the future, it built a new sanctuary and a manse. It lasted until 1857 when external controversies and internal divisions led to the withdrawal of one quarter of the membership to found the Reformed Church.

The second congregation, the Town Church, grew up with the Metuchen area in the post Civil War period, modernized its structure, expanded its Christian education programs, and created the first organizations for women's activities. Beginning in 1877, it was led by a strong pastor, Rev. James Mason, until the second decade of the twentieth century, when his interest in the reform cause of prohibition of alcoholic beverages came to override his responsibilities to his congregation, and its vitality gradually drained away in the 1920s.

The third congregation, the Suburban Church, was forecast in 1931 with the construction of the Educational Building to accommodate rising enrollment in its church school. It flowered dramatically in the great ingathering of members from the 1940s through the 1960s, when its membership briefly reached a peak of 2,300. Again led by a strong pastor, Rev. Adolph Behrenberg, it created the staff and congregational leadership, the physical plant, and the programs and services to sustain itself. But it faded rapidly in the 1970s amid the social and political turmoil of the times, and the pastor's own disillusionment with efforts to stem the forces of decline.

The fourth congregation, the Urban Church, was born in the 1980s, developed a new sense of mission and outreach, and is with us today. This congregation is more informal in its ways, more democratic in its leadership, more energetic in inventing new programs, and concerned not only with receiving the inspiration of its worship services, but also

11

involved in what is done in its name in the community. It also shares the love of God with each other, ministering within the congregation in a variety of ways, and holding up a strong sense of family participation in its activities.

No church exists in isolation; it fulfills its mission through its links to the world around it. As it affects the life of the community, so also the forces of change affect the church itself. The history of each of these congregations demonstrates a pattern of renewal, success and decline that reflects different periods of American history. In this context, renewal refers sometimes to external circumstances, such as recovery from a period of war opening into a time of new beginnings. It also refers to the willingness of the congregation to begin again, to renew its commitment to Christian service and to strike out in new ways to accomplish it. Success refers to the continued vitality of its activities over an extended period of time to carry out its mission. Decline, like renewal, can refer to external circumstances, and it also refers to a loss of purpose and a time of drifting, until a new vision of mission takes hold.

We will see in this history that three of the four congregations arose out of a time of renewal that accompanied the transition from war to peace, in the American Revolution, the Civil War, and World War II. The fourth congregation, our own, came out of an equally turbulent time of social disruption and the search for a new sense of community. Similarly, two congregations declined at a time of national division and controversy, over slavery and Civil War in the mid-nineteenth century and over civil rights and the Vietnam War in the mid-twentieth century. All of our previous congregations benefited from growth and development in the community and nation, and all experienced the severance of the link between pastor and congregation.

These forces are not necessarily exclusive of one another. Efforts at renewal can occur during a period of success, helping to keep the congregation adjusting its mission endeavors. Evidence of decline can weaken and undermine its mission, and then be successfully overcome to resume a further period of growth. It is also true, of course, that the congregation is a continuous body, and therefore many members lived through the transitions between the various congregations. Many members of our present congregation, for instance, were also members of the Suburban Church.

In order to examine the experience of each of the four congregations to see how this pattern of renewal, success and decline works out, we will disregard historical chronology in order better to highlight the differences and similarities among them. In chapters two and three, we will first relate the spectacular growth of the Suburban Church under its pastor, Dr. Behrenberg, then its equally steep decline in numbers in the 1970s under the battering effect of the social conflicts over civil rights and the Vietnam War. In chapter four, we will consider the history of the Town Church, its immediate predecessor, with a similar experience, on a much smaller scale. It, too, grew up with the Borough of Metuchen in an earlier era under the guidance of a strong pastor, Rev. James Mason, and then lost its way as its pastor developed other interests.

In chapter five, the rise of our present congregation out of a new search for community and the development of a very different mission oriented congregation will bring us up to date. Finally, in chapter six, we will look back at our first congregation, the Village Church, with its similar experience of confronting a risky future with a congregation, like ours, willing to take new steps in mission outreach. It makes an interesting story. It will conclude with some observations about the place, the mission, and the time span of these congregations.

Chapter II

THE SUBURBAN CHURCH, 1929-1967

Renewal and Success

The seeds of our third congregation were sown in the late twenties, but its full impact was delayed until the late forties by the economic effects of the 1930s depression and the manpower requirements of World War II. A new minister, Rev. George Humphries, came in 1925; Session was reorganized to put an elder in charge of each of eight divisions: advertising, visitation, prayer meetings, Sunday school, Christian endeavor, evening service, brotherhood and music. Membership began to grow, reaching 400 from 1929 into the 1930s and Sunday school enrollment reached 250. To accommodate the latter, plans were laid in 1930 to build a new two story brick educational building. The project was quickly accomplished, and the building dedicated on June 14, 1931. It was the first new church building in more than eighty years, planned and carried out in the midst of economic depression. In order to attract more adults and youth into membership, the congregation created a board of religious education in 1941.

The adverse impact of the depression in loss of employment and widespread poverty attracted the pastor's efforts to an immediate need for helpfulness and spiritual guidance to the community at large. He conducted a large, community wide Men's Bible Class, and served without pay as the borough's first welfare director, supplying basic needs of coal and food for people who could not do so on their own. Church operations, meanwhile, were hampered by declining income; the pastor's salary was cut, and necessary maintenance on the manse postponed. On the national scene, the expanding role of the federal government in the 1930s provided for social security, unemployment insurance, recognition of labor unions, and economic recovery for business and banking. The growth of job opportunities in the 1940s along with mobilization required by participation in World War II pointed the way out of depression. By the end of the war, a more mobile and more prosperous society, newly caught up in the exhilarating victory over Germany and Japan, eagerly reaching out to resume an old life or start a new one, heralded a time of renewal. The church was about to be caught up in a great expansion of numbers, programs and building.

In 1941, a report from Presbytery pointed out the need for more suburban churches to meet the needs of a population shifting to the suburbs. Dr. Adolph Behrenberg was called as pastor in September 1942. By 1945 membership stood at 675, about double what it was only four years before. The need for more space to carry on church activities was apparent. At a congregation meeting in 1945, a proposal to build a "parish hall" was adopted, to include an auditorium, dining room and kitchen, to be located in the orchard between the manse and the church. A finance committee and a building committee were appointed, and the congregation undertook to raise the expected cost of $30,000 in three years. Construction was completed promptly and the social center was dedicated on October 24, 1948. Its expectation to unite church and community and to serve as a gathering place for people of all ages was quickly fulfilled. In 1956, a new west wing was added to provide needed office space.

Another outreach into the community occurred in 1949 with the organization of a Community Nursery School, sponsored at first by the Evening Circle and then by the 20-30 Club. Beginning with eighteen children that fall, it rapidly established itself as a nondenominational service to the community.

The population of the Metuchen area grew rapidly in the late forties and fifties. Census figures indicate that Metuchen's population, around 2,000 early in the century, passed 10,000 early in the 1950s, and reached 14,000 by 1960. In the same decade of the fifties, Edison almost tripled its population, and the population of Piscataway doubled. The population of the three towns was about 35,000 in 1950, 80,000 in 1960 and over 110,000 in 1970. The growth in our neighboring towns has continued in more recent decades. Even by the end of 1950, more members had been received in the eight years preceeding than had occurred in the entire 48-year ministry of Rev. Mason. By the spring of 1951 more than 1,000 had joined the church in Dr. Behrenberg's ministry; from 1949 on, the total membership was never under 1,000. The pastor himself was the chief recruiter, making calls on residents as soon as they moved into the area, inviting them to come to church. People joined to be with friends and for the fellowship that represented a renewed community after the separation brought on by wartime employment and military service. The great ingathering continued into the 1960s, doubling the membership again, and the energies of the congregation were necessarily absorbed in developing programs and services to sustain large numbers. A recent book (John Judis, "The Paradox of American Democracy") called the 1950s the great American celebration of prosperity and democracy, with rising incomes, home ownership, and suburban life style. That was the heart of the Suburban church.

A weekly Parish News, written by the pastor, began in September 1948, and by the next spring its circulation was nearly 600 homes. It brought information about church activities, individual members, committee meetings, special events, and messages from Presbytery. Fellowship was encouraged by a schedule of Parish Nights on the second Friday of each month, with different groups in the church sponsoring the entertainment. One of the most active of these groups was the 20-30 Club, a gathering of friends around the pastor, who was a bachelor, and providing

17

much of the lay leadership for the church and its programs over a span of twenty years, 1947-1967. Reflecting the values of its time, the club emphasized fellowship, friendship and leadership.

In 1953, Rev. Ben Whitaker, who had been hired as assistant minister four years earlier, became the first associate pastor on the staff, with responsibility for youth, confirmation class, released time (Friday afternoon activities for grades one through six), and regular parish calling. He also preached during the summer months when the pastor was away. In 1955, Margaret Condon was hired to fill the new position of Director of Christian Education; she carried out that responsibility for the next fifteen years.

That same year, with membership about 1,400, double sessions of both church (9:30 AM and 11 AM) and Sunday school began. A new organ was installed and dedicated on October 30, 1955. Communion was served the first Sunday of each month at the 9:30 AM service. In 1956, enrollment in the Sunday school, including both students and teachers, almost reached 1,000 a fourfold increase in the last ten years. Other special services were added: 7:30 PM Christmas Eve in 1957 and 10 PM in 1962. The traditional midnight service had begun in 1942. An 8 AM Easter service was added to the traditional 6 AM sunrise service in 1958 and a service on Good Friday in 1959.

The constantly rising number of people required more space, and planning began in 1957 for the largest building and renovation project ever undertaken. The final plans included expansion of the Educational Building to include eight new classrooms and additional office space, the exterior of the church covered in brick, a new bell tower and steeple, reconstruction of the narthex to include choir rooms and cloakrooms, a new Session room and a new Chapel. A professional fundraiser was engaged to raise $250,000. Groundbreaking occurred in a snowstorm in mid-February 1958; in April the congregation began using the Forum Theater for worship services. The cornerstone was laid October 5 and the new facilities dedicated December 14, 1958. All of these new additions were used to full capacity right from the start.

By 1967 the Suburban Church was ready to celebrate the 250th anniversary of its founding. Its membership reached a peak of 2,300 in 1967 and 1968. Church school enrollment peaked at 175 teachers and 1,200 children and youth. Young people in the Confirmation class numbered around 50 each year; half the class was confirmed on Maundy Thursday, half on Good Friday. The focus of this extraordinary effort was the pastor himself, the symbol of the Suburban Church, sustained by Session and Trustees and by the loyalty of lay leadership. This congregation was homogeneous, middle class, well educated, commuting business and professional people, with a home-owning suburban life style.

It was the pastor's summer trips that kept the congregation aware of the outside world. Dr. Behrenberg emphasized the need to relate one's religious beliefs and attitudes to world issues and problems. His summer trips always ended with his eagerly awaited post-Labor Day sermon on "Religious and Allied Observations Following a Trip," and the series of fall lectures, many with slides, that attracted a wide audience. By the 1960s, he had visited 105 countries, and had made seven trips around the world. In 1957 the benevolence budget first included the United Mission Hospital in Nepal. The total budget for benevolence grew from $1,500 in 1941 to $31,000 in 1965, and the overall budget for church operations from $8,000 to $96,000.

In the 1960s and 1970s, as it turned out, the world that was clamoring for attention was not far away, it was right outside the walls of the church. A hint of what was to come happened a few years earlier with the assassination of President John F. Kennedy, which brought a spontaneous gathering of a shocked congregation to a prayer meeting on Friday evening, November 22, 1963. Earlier that summer, a massive civil rights rally in Washington was energized by the inspiring voice of Rev. Martin Luther King, Jr., and the demand for legislation was fulfilled in 1964 and

1965 with laws to outlaw racial discrimination and to protect voting rights. Violence erupted over the efforts to carry out the promise of racial harmony. The murder of three civil rights workers in Mississippi, who were arrested by a sheriff's deputy and turned over to the Ku Klux Klan, led to many rallies across the nation, one of which occurred in the Metuchen church on August 30, 1964. One of the speakers was Ben Chaney, the 12-year-old brother of one of the murdered victims. Even as planning for the 1967 celebration was taking place, the world outside was beginning to experience the shock of the struggle for racial justice that erupted in 1967 in urban rioting and property destruction that reached as close as Plainfield and New Brunswick. For this congregation, the road ahead looked dangerous and unpredictable.

Chapter III

THE SUBURBAN CHURCH, 1967-1979

Shock and Response

In the fall of 1967, the congregation celebrated the 250th anniversary of its founding in 1717 with a series of six worship services and a congregational banquet. Systematic planning for the celebration had begun in 1962, under the direction of a large committee co-chaired by Richard Hale and Saxon Palmeter. Four of the Sunday services that fall were given twice, at 9:30 AM and 11 AM in accordance with the schedule in effect since 1955.

The Service of Dedication on September 10, 1967, included the burning of the mortgage on the social center and the rededication of the church itself, "restored and beautified." On September 17, 1967, the 25th anniversary service of the pastor was identified as a "service for the re-consecration of the services of the pastor." On October 8, 1967, the 250th anniversary service included a note about the number of pastors who had served the congregation, including only three in the ninety years since 1877. The accumulated service of the three, Rev. Mason, Rev. Humphries and Rev. Behrenberg, was to extend to a full century by the time of Dr. Behrenberg's death in 1977. The sermon at this service was given by William Phelps Thompson, Stated Clerk of the United Presbyterian Church in the U.S.A.

A week later at 8 PM came the 20th anniversary concert in honor of the organist, Gretchen Iobst. The concert featured the choir cantata, "Psalm

21

of Redemption," by Robert Elmore, organist and composer, who was in the audience. The cantata included the hymn, "Most Holy Lord and God," with music provided for the congregation to join in the last verse.

On October 22, 1967, at 4 PM an Ecumenical Service was held, with eleven clergy from various Metuchen churches participating. The sermon was given by the Rev. Kenneth Walter, stated Clerk of the Presbytery of Elizabeth, and the program included prayers for the unity of the church, for the nation and for peace, and the offering was given for the "suffering people of Vietnam and the Middle East." The last of the services, on October 29, 1967, was in commemoration of the 450th anniversary of the beginning of the Protestant Reformation, an anniversary that Dr. Behrenberg particularly delighted in associating with the anniversary of the Metuchen church.

Earlier on Saturday evening, September 30, 1967, a congregational banquet was held at Rutgers University Commons in New Brunswick. About 600 attended, some brief historical skits were given, and the recently published history of the church was distributed to the members present.

The celebration throughout that fall centered on the achievements of the present and the benchmarks of the past. People had joined the church for fellowship, for sharing the enthusiasm of growth and prosperity, for creating together the resources for accommodating a large number of people in church and in community, and they eagerly accepted and supported the leadership of their pastor. Unfortunately, the celebration was not used to meet new challenges or to chart a road to the future. The congregation did make some effort to respond to new challenges, but the problems proved overwhelming, and in the 1970s the congregation lost its way and the numbers began declining.

The Church and Society Committee, under the dedicated leadership of Guida West, developed a Covenant of Open Occupancy in 1966, and requested realtors to observe its provisions against discrimination in real estate sales. In 1970 the committee sponsored the first Annual Brotherhood Dinner, in cooperation with the Metuchen-Edison Race Relations Commission. President Lyndon Johnson's Report on a society divided by civil disorder was the subject of discussion in a group including the men's clubs of the Temple and the Methodist Church.

After extensive planning for a youth mission project, in the summer of 1965, a group of fifteen youths and five adults journeyed to the First and Olivet Presbyterian Church in an inner city area of Wilmington, Delaware, to spend a week painting and redecorating the interior of the church. They gave a report on their mission at a worship service in July. Unfortunately, planned subsequent trips had to be cancelled because of the threat of violence in the area. Nevertheless, this activity was an important forecast of what was to come when the mission minded youth of the 1990s linked up with Habitat for Humanity. In August 1965, a sermon by Richard Killmer, seminary assistant, was entitled, "Freedom Now," with the Call to Worship repeating the words of the freedom song, "How Many Roads Must a Man Walk Down Before People Call Him a Man?"

Television brought the struggle for civil rights into the nation's living rooms, with images of marches and demonstrations, police brutality, freedom riders, and the burning of inner cities. Closer to home, in 1967, there was serious racial conflict and property destruction in both Newark and Plainfield, with threatened outbreaks in New Brunswick and rumors that Metuchen would soon have its turn.

In the 1970s the war in Vietnam became highly controversial, in sharp contrast to national public support given to earlier war efforts. On the campus of Kent State University in Ohio, the burning of the ROTC building in May 1970, brought the intervention of armed force and the killing of four students and the wounding of nine. Campus protests erupted nation wide. Compounding the divisions created by these fault lines came the Watergate break-in, the resignation of Vice-President Spiro Agnew in 1973 for accepting kickbacks, and the unprecedented

23

resignation of President Richard Nixon in 1974 under threat of impeachment. The position of every president since has been undermined by distrust, an unfortunate legacy in a constitutional system which depends on national elections. The climate of optimism and the confidence in democracy that had characterized the 1950s was giving way to bitterness and disillusionment.

The impact of these events on the Suburban Congregation was swift and sudden, almost as a tidal wave overrunning the church. During a period of ten years, 1969-1979, steady declines were recorded in church attendance, church membership, church school enrollment and budget receipts. Double sessions ended in 1973 and the position of Director of Christian Education was eliminated. In 1974, Session was reduced from twenty-one to eighteen and communion reduced to eight times a year. Overall membership steadily declined, to 1,939 in 1972, 1,581 in 1975, 1,350 in 1977, a loss of over 40 percent. Church school enrollment fell under 1,000 in 1968, to 658 in 1970, 543 in 1972 and 478 in 1975, a 60 percent loss. Declines continued at a somewhat slower pace into the 1980s. In the longer perspective from the middle sixties to the middle eighties, church school enrollment declined by 80 percent, overall membership by 50 percent. The core that remained became the foundation of the Urban Congregation of the 80s and 90s.

Meanwhile, other events occurred which were important for the future. In 1973 the mortgage on the second manse was paid off and the church became debt free for the first time since 1948. In 1972 Rev. Richard Avery of the Port Jervis, New York Presbyterian Church and his choir director, Donald Marsh, visited the church and helped with the dedication of the banners illustrating the confessions of the church. The banners had been made by women in the congregation to specifications provided by Avery and Marsh, who designed the symbols. And in 1976, through the efforts of the Palmeter family, working through Church World Service, the congregation began the sponsorship of two Vietnamese refugees to help them settle into the community and find jobs. These activities were a small but significant forecast of the mission-minded congregation that was soon to emerge. But the true response to new needs would await a new time and a new congregation. The Suburban Church and its pastor hung on to the secure past; it had no adequate answer to the frightening future. Dr. Behrenberg fell ill in the fall of 1977, and early on the morning of December 30th he died, marking the end of the Suburban Church. The Chapel memorializes his life.

What legacy did this congregation pass on to its successor? The building of the social center and the organization of the Community Nursery School enabled the church to reach out into its community and provided a place for people to meet. The Suburban Church passed on to its successor a debt-free church; a core membership that never dipped below 1,000; an ability to organize effective programs; services, staff and building space to carry a large congregation; and strong programs in music and Christian Education. It maintained a successful program of stewardship through the Every Member Canvass enabling it to increase its budget to keep up with its commitments. It had extended its mission reach overseas and created precedents for future mission activity. It had also successfully aided the formation of the Edison Community Church in 1952, and the Oak Tree Church in 1965. And it had provided a Chinese Christian congregation with temporary space in the social center while it searched for a permanent home. Finally, there is the story of John Thompson, whose family came to Metuchen from Virginia in the 1920s. Thompson became the caretaker for the church, living in the small white cottage behind the church next to the cemetery. The New Hope Baptist Church was first organized in the living room of that cottage, and in 1946 its new congregation had enough money to buy land on Hampton Street, where it is presently located.

Chapter IV

THE TOWN CHURCH, 1858-1928

Out of the disruption of church life brought on by the struggle over slavery, secession and Civil War, a period of renewal began to herald a new congregation. It took some time to put church operations in order again, and involved some discarding of old ways, and creating new ones. Pew rent collection ended in 1859; collection for benevolence began to be held on the third Sunday of each month in support of Presbyterian Board of Foreign Missions, the Board of Education and the American Bible Society. An envelope system providing for weekly contributions was in place in the early seventies, and Session made efforts to increase collections by annual visitation of members. Sunday evening services began, as well as a Wednesday evening prayer meeting.

What was later to become the Borough of Metuchen as a trading and transportation center was clearly taking shape in the 1870s as a variety of businesses became established along the west side of Main Street. That development, plus the final location of the railroad station at Main Street instead of Lake Avenue began to define the central downtown area. Metuchen was also acquiring a reputation as a desirable residential area of the surrounding Raritan Township. Rev. James Mason, the long-term pastor of the Town Church, actively encouraged writers, editors and artists from New York to take up residence. A new reading room was opened in 1870 by the Sons of Temperance. In the membership of the Town

Church, farmers still predominated, but there were also professional people, businessmen and skilled laborers.

Protestantism in general was at a high point of its prestige between 1875 and the First World War. There was great interest in improving Christian education and expanding Sunday school curricula. New organizations, like the Christian Endeavor Society, founded in 1881, rapidly expanded its membership across the country, putting emphasis on youth programs of worship, study and recreation beyond Sunday school. The beginning of the Chatauqua movement in 1874 in New York State was motivated by the need to train Sunday school teachers in their increasing responsibilities. For the Town Church concern for the instruction of children was seen as a way to recruit new members for the congregation. Sunday school classes were divided into separate departments, based on age, and separate curricula developed for each department. The church found it difficult to find space to house these and other increased activities. Friday evening prayer meetings were held in what were called the "outposts" of the congregation, in New Durham, Bonhamtown, Oak Tree, and Menlo Park. One Sunday school class met for a time in the small railroad station at Menlo Park. All this inconvenience was regarded as worthwhile, nevertheless; Presbytery meetings came to be highlighted by the reports of individual churches about their Christian Education enrollment and programs.

The social gospel movement became popular in these years, emphasizing the need for social reform to overcome the evils of society. For Presbyterians, that meant temperance, keeping the Sabbath, and outlawing gambling. It also meant that new immigrant groups with different ideas about the recreational use of Sundays and the importance of saloons did not flock to Presbyterian churches, especially in suburban areas and small towns. Stewardship in meeting local church needs as well as mission giving was also given new importance.

For the Town Church, mission gradually became important, both at home and abroad, though sometimes in incidental ways. Mission giving was encouraged by Rev. Mason, who said in one of his sermons, "As Christ broke the loaves and distributed them, so must we break ourselves and distribute our good doing, through the widest circle of the world." Some money left over from the Anti-Race Track Fund was sent to the relief of suffering farmers in Nebraska. A small balance in the Deacons Fund was used to purchase temperance books for the church library. Much more important for mission projects were the women's organizations that sprang up in the last two decades of the nineteenth century. The Young Ladies Home Missionary Society, founded in 1879, made clothing and other material for schools and missions in various parts of the country, and even contributed to teachers' salaries in several states. The Ladies Aid Society, organized in 1888, undertook to raise money for the needs of the local church. Through sewing and quilting bees, and an Annual Strawberry and Ice Cream Festival, the society helped to pay the salaries of the organist and the sexton. Over the years, contributions were made toward a new roof for the church, new lamps and a new carpet, and the society frequently paid the church's coal bills. Beginning in 1896 the Women's Guild sponsored an Annual Bazaar in the fall and its fundraising helped in keeping church facilities in good repair. The young mothers of the Guild brought their children to meetings and parked their baby carriages outside the meeting room. The Guild also enjoyed a friendly rivalry with the Men's Brotherhood, founded in 1908. Its collection of $100 at a minstrel show performance in 1914 was donated to the Borough for the construction of sidewalks along the west side of Main Street. In the 1920s, the Guild undertook the major task of providing new cushions and new curtains for the church.

Session was kept busy in coordinating all the fundraising activities and maintaining the physical plant. A new organ was installed in 1908, following earlier installation of stained glass windows and the recasting of the church bell. To emphasize the importance of systematic giving, an envelope system specifically for benevolence was established in 1909; in 1917 an Every-Member Canvass made 110 family visits on one Sunday afternoon.

Festival days, besides Christmas and Easter, included Rally Day in September, Harvest Home in November, Children's Day and an annual picnic in the spring. A major church event was the commissioning of the pastor's daughter, Irene, as missionary to India in 1914, and her marriage to the Rev. Arthur Harper, which occurred just before their departure for India. In October 1916, the centennial celebration of the Sunday school involved the participation of almost 200 students and teachers. It was one of the high points in the history of the Town Church.

In 1912 and 1913, Rev. Mason's interest in temperance and prohibition of alcoholic beverages began to intensify and to consume most of his energies for the next decade. Participating in the activities of the Prohibition Party, leading a successful campaign for prohibition in Metuchen, and running unsuccessfully for political office became the focus of his life. As a result, collections declined, and pastoral work needed on a daily basis was not happening. The interests of the pastor and his congregation diverged, and it broke the connection needed to sustain the Town Church. As if to mark the end of an era, two of the long-time lay leaders of the church died in 1920. R. Bruce Crowell had served as Clerk of Session for thirty-three years; C. C. Campbell had been a trustee for fifty-four years and superintendent of the Sunday school for thirty years. By the early 1920s, the Town Church found itself adrift and without purpose. Rev. Mason's pastorate finally limped to a close in 1925. He lived on in Metuchen until 1938. A plaque in his memory is mounted on the rear wall of the sanctuary.

The congregation of the Town Church contributed to its successor an ability to grow with its community and provide for the long-term growth and maintenance of its physical plant and the programs that it particularly valued. The congregation made Christian education for all ages a major priority, a foundation on which both of its successor congregations built. An important legacy was the organization and ongoing work of women's groups, to carry on the serious beginnings of mission work, fundraising to support various needs, and teaching Sunday school classes. There were also strict limitations on women's opportunities for leadership in the church. Women were not allowed to become pastors, or to preach, or to serve on Session. Not until the 1930s were women permitted to earn degrees at Princeton Seminary. As it turned out, this was just the beginning of a long twentieth century struggle until the 1980s when women finally began to reach their full potential for church leadership. Finally, the Town Church and its successor, the Suburban Church, were closely linked to the fortunes of their long-term pastors, and when those fortunes faltered, both congregations lost their way.

Chapter V

THE URBAN CHURCH, 1980-2000

Rebuilding a Community

Turmoil and disruption of established customs accompanied the birth of the fourth congregation, the Urban Church. Stable family relationships were radically changed by the rise in divorce rates after 1965. The entry of women into the job market on a permanent basis, and advances in medical technology made career and family planning both possible but sometimes hard to manage. The newly formed National Organization for Women stimulated efforts to end discrimination, both sexual and racial, in a struggle for equal pay and equal opportunity that still goes on. In fact, at the dawn of a new century, the battle for civil rights and the struggle against discrimination have engendered new causes that are being fought out on many fronts, including churches, and the legacy of the seventies in distrust of government and tension between public and private are strongly affecting the political process. We are still trying to clear up the debris scattered across the landscape a quarter century ago. The Urban Church arose out of a desire to create a new sense of community in a world where individualism had gotten out of control. It offered new ways to instill values for families and children. It provided ways to help neighbors and those in need. It brought the vision of tearing down the walls of the church, to reach out in mission activity that would engage its adult and youth population. It offered spiritual guidance in sermon and bible study, and concern for people who were coping with serious crises in their lives. So arose a congregation that learned how to work together, pray together, and seek God's calling for their lives. Beginning in the ministries of Rev. Robert Bayley and Rev. Joyce Rife, it is reaching toward its full development in the ministry of Rev. Robert Beringer. Joyce Rife completed her ministry in July 1984 to move with her family to Atlanta. As she walked out the door, Bob walked in, to begin his ministry with us on August 1, 1984. The congregation meeting approving the pastor's call was held on June 3, 1984, exactly to the day the 200th anniversary of the first recorded congregation meeting of the Metuchen church.

Even though many families in the earlier Suburban Church continue as members of the Urban Church, there are great differences between the two. Part of the contrast can be seen in the Church Information Forms drawn up in 1978, resulting in the call to Rev. Bayley, and in 1991, resulting in the call to Rev. Lucia Jackson. Average church attendance in 1991 was 340, about 34 percent of the membership. In 1978, church attendance was 290, only 19 percent of the membership at that time. The church budget in 1991 was $498,000; in 1978, with a larger membership, only $155,000. Mission giving had increased ten times in 1991 over 1981.

Other differences also offer a sharp contrast. There are now a large number of children present at worship, singing in children's choirs and gathering for the children's sermon, which had begun in a small way in the summer of 1980. Children's bulletins for the Sunday service began to be provided in 1988. At church services in the earlier Suburban Congregation, there were no children. The Annual Summer Adventure Club Program, begun in 1987 to take the place of Vacation Bible School, and in recent years carried out in cooperation with personnel from the Reformed Church, has attracted many children from families that are not church members.

There are now women in established positions of leadership. Rev. Joyce Rife was our first woman associate pastor, 1982-1984. She was succeeded by Rev. Lark Zunich, 1985-1990, Rev. Lucia Jackson, 1990-

1995, and Rev. Barbara Aspinall in 1995-1996. Rev. Karen Chamis began her ministry with us in 1996, until she accepted another call in the fall of 2000. More recently, Rev. Heather Finck served as associate in ministry until May 2000. Brenda Day has been Minister of Music since 1993 and Marilyn Tyrrell has brought expert leadership to several of the handbell choirs. Women have been prominent in positions of Director of Children's Ministries and Sunday school Superintendent. Women are well represented on the Unicameral Board and its various commissions and committees, and of course, on the Board of Deacons. Our seminary representatives have frequently been women, and in 1999-2000, we were served by a couple, Matt and Melinda Hoyt, who are caring for a newborn child. By contrast, in the earlier Suburban Congregation, there was only Gretchen Iobst as Minister of Music and Margaret Condon as Director of Christian Education. Until 1966, there were no women on Session and all the ministers were male. The great value of women's participation in leadership, enhanced by the activities of Presbyterian Women, has been an important part of the family orientation of the Urban Congregation.

Social and economic characteristics of the two congregations are also quite different. In 1978 the congregation was described as 99 percent white, 60 percent college educated, and 90 percent living in private homes. By 1991, the congregation was experiencing the first group of its Indonesian members, and black and Hispanic members were increasing. The economic basis of the congregation in 1991 was considerably more varied in employment, housing, and two-income families. Our congregation has also been enriched by new members coming from different religious backgrounds. Worship services include family groups, youth, single men and women, and elderly members. Bread served at communion is now cut from a variety of loaves, symbolizing that diversity.

A community of faith is at work here, reaching out in mission, caring for each other, learning the Bible and responding to spiritual guidance. People join to become an active part of that community. Mission to the immediate community is carried out through the Local Assistance Fund and the Food Bank, first organized in 1984, and through the Board of Deacons. In 1989, the Shared Living project for assisted living facilities began to be developed; named the Beringer House, honoring the pastor's active leadership in the project, it opened in 1993. The monthly ministry to Birchwood Nursing and Convalescent Center began in October 1989, as did the mission committee's provision of a monthly meal to the homeless families at the Ozanam Shelter in Edison. Support for the families at Amandla Crossing has recently been added.

Farther afield, the first link with Habitat for Humanity was made by Rev. Lucia Jackson in 1991 to work in Hartford, Connecticut, in 1992 in Vermont and in 1993 in Circleville, West Virginia. These annual summer mission trips for youth and adults have continued in New Hampshire and Pennsylvania, giving invaluable experience in helping others build and renovate homes, and providing valuable insight on how that experience connects to one's faith journey. As one youth participant put it some years ago, "It makes you realize you have to give something of yourself"; and from a more recent participant, "My strength grows when I help others." These are truly Christian lives at work. By the end of the decade, these mission trips attracted twice the number of youth and adults as the Wilmington trip of 1965 — this from a congregation only half as large.

Making up and delivering holiday food baskets to needy families at Thanksgiving, Christmas and Easter has become a bigger project almost every year. An important part of mission endeavor is "hands on" mission projects conducted at various times of the year. The best example is the Advent Workshop began by Bob and Peggy Beringer in the first year of his ministry. In addition to the increased mission budget, the congregation helps with fundraising projects carried out by youth and by the senior choir for their particular summer mission trips. The importance of all this mission activity to the congregation brought a recent remark from Rev. Heather Finck that it was "a true blessing to do ministry with a congregation that is so committed to outreach and mission, both within its community and beyond."

Caring for each other got a boost in the early eighties when Rev. Rife set up a Visitation Commission, as she began to realize that an increasing number of her parishioners needed personal kinds of help in their lives. The work of this commission was an important forerunner of the more structured Stephen Minister program, begun in 1995-1996 under the leadership of Rosalind Docs, Donald Lee and Darlene Kline, to bring Christian caring and love to individuals suffering through crises in their lives. The Deacons Blood Bank began in 1984, and the ongoing sickroom equipment supply project also got underway.

The strong feeling that this congregation bears responsibility for the programs it supports has periodically led to new endeavors. A monthly Saturday morning workplace connection breakfast began in 1997. The Social Issues Committee set up a Parenting Group, and a valuable Parish Nursing Program was recently established. In 1986, a men's breakfast group started, called Eggs and Inspiration. It attracted a large group to a series of programs on Christian ethics in business, sports, medicine and other areas. In time the program turned into a men's luncheon group, which meets monthly at the Cornerstone Restaurant. An important part of caring for each other is the prominent role played by the Board of Deacons, whose responsibilities in this congregation have expanded greatly from its predecessors. Board members, divided into teams, now deliver flowers, visit home-bound parishioners, assist in services at Birchwood Nursing Home, make and deliver a monthly meal to the Ozanam Shelter, conduct a blood drive and raise some of their own funds with an annual chicken barbecue.

To foster more Bible study, the first Lenten Devotional Booklet was prepared by Rev. Lark Zunich in 1986; subsequently, church members, following instructions and suggestions, contributed their own biblical thoughts and prayers. To further support this effort, Share Your Faith Night, during Lent, began in 1995, offering opportunities for parishioners to tell of their own faith journeys. In 1997, the Adult Education Committee began a monthly Moment for the Bible, given by individual members of the Sunday worship service. Responding to answers to a questionnaire circulated by the Women's Association in 1986, Rev. Lark Zunich started the Young Mothers and Others bible study group; over the years it has changed its focus and composition; now called Moms on Monday, it meets a continuing need for mothers with young children. Bible study groups are carried on by Presbyterian Women (its official name since 1989), and recently by our husband and wife team from Seminary. The pastor conducts one weekly and one twice-a-month bible study. Rev. Rife began the Tenebrae Service during Holy Week in 1983, and it has become one of the most spiritually moving services of the year. More recently, a monthly Service of Wholeness has been added.

The role of the pastor in the Urban Church is very different from what it was in the earlier congregation. It was aptly forecast in the early 1990s in interviews with various people as to what role religion would play in American life in the twenty-first century. One scholar forecast "a roll up your sleeves, helping people in a practical sense religion." People would be doing something about homelessness, hunger, toxic waste, and the environment. A prominent clergyman thought the century would bring a recovery of our religious roots to sustain human values in a secular world. The spiritual leader would be less a program director, and more a spiritual guide to people in their own walk of faith, and this would result in a more loving and caring congregation. But, for us, it's more than that. Our pastor keeps us focused on the central core of our faith, to open our hearts to the love of Christ, and to let Christ be the motivator who leads us in our daily mission. Then he lets things happen.

In this Urban Congregation, we are doing these things now, amid a sense of joy and excitement that is also apparent. There is a buzz of conversation as members gather on Sunday morning, and there is frequently laughter responding during a sermon. The serious challenge of our faith is there, too, whether the biblical admonitions to keep us focused on how to live our lives, or the welcome to a newly baptized child, or the appreciation of applause that occasionally responds to a choir performance. We are all participating, we are all responding, and sometimes we are all leading. At the annual meeting of the congregation in June 1999, held in the social center while the sanctuary was being repainted, Bob Beringer's fifteenth anniversary as pastor was recognized as members of the Pastor Nominating Committee that called him came to the front of the auditorium. In the comments that were then made by various people, one parishioner rose to say, "Bob, you have made this *our* church." Exactly so. And now we have the scary responsibility of making sure we participate and provide the lay leadership and other resources to continue to make it happen in the future.

The early efforts made by Director of Music, Sandra West, to stimulate interest in the music program of the church were greatly aided, through the generosity of George Evans, by the donation of a set of handbells in 1981, along with funds to buy music and equipment, and for training leaders. In the years that followed the number of bell choirs and singing choirs grew rapidly under the leadership of Brenda Day, involving children, youth and adults, giving the music program a prominent role in the congregation's activities. It is also an important part of mission, as bell choirs visit schools and nursing homes, and the senior choir distributed Bibles on its trips abroad in 1996 and 2000. The long process of upgrading and renovating the church organ was undertaken in the 1980's under the guidance of Brenda Day and Bill Kistler working with representatives of the Austin Organ Company, which had installed the instrument in 1955. A capital fund drive supported this effort, and in 1985 Brenda and Bill gave a harpsichord and organ concert, in observance of the 300th anniversary of the birth of Johann Sebastian Bach. Presently, further changes are being undertaken, including an upgrading of the organ console, and a

39

new carillon for the bell tower. With contributions from members, the new Presbyterian Hymnal was installed for use in 1990, and new pew Bibles were purchased in 1998.

The church as been blessed with growing financial resources. The second manse was sold in 1982, and major legacies received more recently have boosted the investment and endowment fund to more than $3,500,000 in 1997. This has made possible the purchase of computing equipment for the church offices, a new sound system in the sanctuary, and the taping of services to make them available to people unable to attend church. Recently a new interior walkway between the sanctuary and the educational building was completed, and the sanctuary repainted. New furnishings and redecoration were carried out in frequently used rooms. A videotape of church operations was prepared by Hannah Kerwin, and used effectively in stewardship drives and in new member's classes.

Finally, the Commission system, started by Rev. Bayley in the early eighties and revised periodically, became the basic structure of decision making, providing opportunities for participation of church members in the numerous committees organized under the Commissions. In 1993, Session and Trustees were merged into a Unicameral Board.

The Lord has blessed this congregation in many ways, and we did not forget to mark certain milestones along our way. In 1986, the first Sunday of February, the sanctuary of the church was rededicated for the 150th anniversary of its building in 1836. In mid-November 1987 at a Saturday evening dinner and a Sunday morning Worship Service, we observed the 200th anniversary of the separation of our "upper congregation" from its mother church in Woodbridge and its incorporation as the Second Presbyterian Church of Woodbridge. In 1991, the 175th anniversary of the Sunday school was noted, and in 1992, the church held an Open House in commemoration of the 275th anniversary of its founding in 1717.

In 1992-1993 we prepared the church's historical records dating back to 1717, and delivered them to the Presbyterian Historical Society in Philadelphia, where they are preserved in temperature and humidity controlled vaults. A microfilm of those records is kept in the church office. It includes minutes of Session, Trustees and Congregation meetings through the eighteenth, nineteenth and the first three decades of the twentieth century, as well as minutes of the women's societies founded in the late nineteenth century, and other miscellaneous documents.

Now at the turn of the century, this family congregation ministers to one another and goes outside beyond the walls of the church into the community near and far, to be an expression of Christ's love for all. Through its long range planning committee, it seeks to make provision for new needs as they arise. We do not know what shocks, internal or external, the church may suffer in the future, amid the fast-paced changes in our society. But if we labor on, with eyes and ears open to God's call, and with peace, love and joy in our hearts, God will be on our side, to be a community of faith and hope, striving always to carry out its mission of service, of justice and loving concern for those in need.

Chapter VI

THE VILLAGE CHURCH, 1787-1857

The program booklet of our 200th anniversary celebration in 1987 reminds us of our heritage. The booklet tells of the congregation meeting in April 1987, held to elect seven members to constitute a Board of Trustees, pursuant to a law of incorporation passed by the newly formed New Jersey State legislature. At a meeting in October of that year, the Trustees incorporated the church as the Second Presbyterian Church of Woodbridge, and in 1799 created a seal with the inscription "2 P. C. of Woodbridge." The program booklet tells of Rev. Azel Roe, pastor of both congregations and strong supporter of the Revolutionary cause. Our anniversary Sunday morning service included a dramatization of events that accompanied the separation, relating to the efforts, eventually futile, of the newly independent congregation to secure a share of the parsonage land. The pew rent list of the congregation showed seventy members, in forty-two pews; in 1792 the meeting house was enlarged to fifty-six pews.

The people in the area had just come through unsettling experiences involving disruption of lives and destruction of property, because of the nearby presence of British and American troops during the war for independence, and constant danger from the larger number of British troops on Staten Island. Peace finally came in 1783, and the state of New Jersey began to organize its own independent government the next year. In the summer of 1787, at a convention in Philadelphia, a new national constitution was written and submitted to the states for ratification. In 1789, as the new nation was inaugurating President George Washington, the Presbyterian Church was also reorganizing its Presbyteries and Synods, and creating a new delegate body, the General Assembly. It was truly a time of new beginnings, a time of renewal, a time to put the past behind and prepare to meet the new challenges of the future.

The little congregation of the Second Church of Woodbridge acted as it did, confident that it would be successful and that the times provided the congregation a new opportunity to bear witness to the ministry of Jesus Christ in its community. The congregation almost stumbled over the lawsuit to gain a share of the parsonage land, but, after overcoming that handicap, called a minister, the Rev. Henry Cook in 1794, who served the church for the next thirty years. Somewhat like our congregation today, this first experiment in church making was congregation driven and was to remain so for the next several decades. For the seventy years of its existence, the Village Church was the only one in the area.

Reacting to inquiries from Presbytery as to what its churches were doing to nurture their children and youth in the Christian faith, the Session decided in 1816 to begin a Sunday school program. Its early classes were held in the old Franklin School House on Middlesex Avenue, which had just been built about a decade before. Robert Ross was the first superintendent. Over the years since 1816, that program has engaged efforts of hundreds of teachers and leaders, and enrolled thousands of young people. It is worthy of note that the Session in taking this action was breaking away from its traditional function of admitting new members and disciplining those already admitted, and taking an important step on the road to becoming the governing body of the church.

Revivalist movements engaged church life in the early nineteenth century, both on the frontier and in more settled areas. During one such occurrence, over sixty new members joined in 1803 and 1804, nearly doubling the membership, to reach 132. The climax of revivalism came in 1818, when 118 new members were admitted during the year, ninety of them on one Sunday in April. Those figures stood unchallenged for over 130 years, until the Suburban Church began to exceed that. One of the new members, Joel Campbell, who subsequently became a Presbyterian minister, wrote that "people would walk two, three and even four miles to attend a prayer meeting." By the end of Henry Cook's ministry in 1824, the membership stood at 202, almost three times its original number. It would not differ greatly over the next hundred years. Rising pew rents made possible an increase in the pastor's salary and the hiring of a chorister to "raise the psalms" in singing.

Increased enrollment demonstrated the need for a larger church building, and plans were initiated by two members who bought land across the road from where the meeting house was located. The congregation made the decision to build a new and larger church, and plans were drawn up in 1835. The coming of the railroad from Newark to New Brunswick at that time accelerated the project and determined exactly where the new building would be located. The new church, modeled after the colonial style church in the town of New Providence, at a total cost of just under $4,000 raised by special subscription, was dedicated on January 30, 1836. Its capacity was about double the size of the membership. Every congregation since then has worshiped in its sanctuary. A decade later, in 1848, the congregation also built the manse at the cost of under $2,400 and carrying a mortgage of $950. With one exception, it has housed every minister who served the church since that time. These achievements were the work of a congregation with a vision of future growth and the faith to achieve it. There was to be no further building program until the construction of the Education Building, more than eighty years later.

The spirit of cooperation among different churches that had characterized early efforts to expand religion in Frontier settlements, and had led to the Plan of Union in 1801 with Congregational churches, began to fragment in the 1830s and 1840s. Doctrinal differences related to the control of frontier mission work, and the requirements for ministerial education in evangelical efforts, led to separation and division. The differences were compounded by differences over slavery. Earlier, the General Assembly in 1818 had called slavery inconsistent with the law of God and the Gospel of Christ, and urged its abolition. But the growing

45

importance of the southern cotton economy, based on slavery and the increasingly violent attacks by abolitionist crusaders, meant that any national church policy was to prove impossible. In 1837 the General Assembly dissolved the Plan of Union and expelled four Synods, which then became the New School Presbyterian Church. The Old School, including the Presbytery of Elizabethtown, expressed fear about the possibility of violent revolution over the slavery question, and its spokesmen began to find authority for defending slavery on scriptural grounds. The two divisions split further into northern and southern components on the eve of the Civil War. They were not to be reunited until 1869.

The Village Church also became mired in its own controversies with two of its pastors, Rev. Holloway Hunt and Rev. Robert Finley, in the 1840s and 1850s. A great deal of bitterness arose between partisans of both sides of what was basically an issue of personality and the exercise of authority within the church. Unfortunately, Presbytery's efforts to reach some resolution only caused more controversy. The result was that in November 1957, fifty-one members withdrew from the congregation with the intention of organizing a new Reformed Church in the community. The loss was about one quarter of the membership, and it marked the end of the career of the Village Church.

In January 1858, the congregation called a new pastor, and in February changed the name of the church to First Presbyterian Church of Metuchen. In a few short years, three more churches, St. Luke's Episcopal, Centenary Methodist, both in 1866, and St. Francis Roman Catholic Church in 1870, were organized. The Village Church, and its colonial predecessor, with a combined 140 years of Christian witness in the community, gave way to its multiple successors. It had bequeathed to its own successor a permanent place in its community, and ability to attract new members to achieve a stable membership of two hundred, an ongoing Sunday school program, and the sanctuary and manse that were to serve it into the far future. Its spirit of risk taking and of reaching out to the community at large was to find an even larger expression in the congregation that is here today.

Chapter VII

THE PLACE, THE MISSION AND THE TIME SPAN

Some concluding observations about this history are worth considering. The four congregations conveniently fall into two pairs. Both the Town Church and the Suburban Church, together stretching across the century from the 1860s to the 1960s, emphasized the development of a strong church that would take its place as a leading institution in its community. Rev. Mason around the turn of the century tried to attract writers, editors and publishers to become residents and church members, and he actively helped to establish the predecessor of the Metuchen public library. He was a friend of Thomas Edison, and provided the church as a place to demonstrate Edison's newly invented phonograph in the 1880s. In his crusade against saloons, he was a well-known person in town. His church offered expanded programs in Christian Education and in new opportunities for women's activities.

In a similar way, the Suburban Church became a leading gathering place. Rev. Behrenberg actively recruited new members; his lectures about his worldwide travels and the world mission of the church attracted a wide audience. Both the social center and the Educational building provided meeting space for many different groups in church and community. With the growth of membership in the 1950s, the church undertook the largest building program in our entire history. The Town Church and the Suburban Church built the walls, opened the doors, and invited people to come in.

In the other pair, our present congregation is very much like the Village Church that began our history. Both the Village Church and the Urban Church emphasized their mission to the community more than their place in it. Working under different pastors, each formed ways, sometimes taking risks to do so, to carry its message of Christian service to the community outside it walls. In effect, they opened the doors, and invited people to go out. Today, we are the beneficiaries of both legacies, with a strong church in its place and a strong mission to the world outside. The responsibilities to maintain that legacy, under Christ's leadership, is ours.

Our second observation relates to the time span of these congregations. Each of the first two congregations lasted about seventy years, the third about fifty. In addition, the span of our colonial experience as an outlying branch of the Woodbridge Church was also about seventy years. All this might suggest that our present congregation, now about twenty years old, will last several more decades into the twenty-first century. We should recognize, however, that the pace of social change since the 1960s and the pace of technological change in the 1990s have substantially accelerated the tempo of life in America. One of the consequences has been an excessive emphasis on individualism and a severe loss of a sense of community. The importance and value of the congregation as a community of faith might come under challenge, perhaps by the attraction of religion on the Internet, or as a consequence of changes in the role of religion in society. While it is impossible to predict what external events may occur, we surely have the privilege now of being in a time of renewal and growth, thankful to God for providing us the means to survive and to carry out our mission to the world outside and to each other. We need to be aware also of the sobering thought that Christ is always calling us anew, to minister to a world that is fractured along many fault lines.

Finally, we should also have deep gratitude to the thousands who came before us, and who took the risks from which we benefit. The next time we gather as a congregation, look around. The sanctuary in which we worship was built by the Village Church, which had the vision to create a space that had more than twice the capacity of its own membership. It began a Sunday school in a building several blocks away. In the midst of economic depression, the early Suburban Church built a new home for the Sunday school, and our programs and activities for youth were first highlighted by the Town Church. In fact, across our entire history, there is an enduring commitment to Christian education. The Suburban Church built the social center, a modern "meeting house." The organization of women's activities began in the Town Church, and the ordination of women elders began in the Suburban church. Mission activities began in small ways in the Town Church, and extended overseas in the Suburban Church.

We can be proud to pass on to our future successors an emphasis on children and families in worship; women in leadership roles, including ordained ministers, a music program, including handbells, that involves people of all ages; a variety of mission activity close to home and through Habitat for Humanity; and a congregation of people with different ethnic and religious backgrounds.

With all these blessings, we can look forward to remembering the legacy of our predecessors at the 175th anniversary of our church sanctuary in 2011, the 225th anniversary of independence from our mother church in 2012, the 200th anniversary of our Sunday school in 2016 and the 300th anniversary of the old meeting house in 2017. And we ourselves have already logged ten years in mission to the Birchwood Nursing Home and Ozanam Shelter, and in the Habitat for Humanity connection.

Praise the Lord for all our blessings!

Chapter VIII

ORIGINS AND EARLY HISTORY
OF THE CHURCH AT WOODBRIDGE

"That in matters of God's worship there shall be liberty of
conscience granted them.... Provided that that liberty granted
shall not extend to licentiousness, nor to disturbance of the
civil peace; and that in every town there shall be allowed 200
acres of land for the maintenance of the Ministry ... there shall
likewise land be allowed for the building of a church, church
yard, and for all other public uses, which are to be exempted
from paying any tax or the Lord's rent of an halfpenny per
acre forever."

– Articles of Agreement, May 21, 1666

As IT APPROACHED its 250th anniversary in 1967, the First Presbyterian Church of Metuchen could count over 2,200 members. It had two
full-time ministers and a student assistant, five major boards supervising
its various activities, a Director of Christian Education, a Director of
Music, and a fully-staffed Church School. Its total receipts approached
$215,000. Most of the breadwinners in its congregation were business
and professional people employed in the vast metropolitan area of central and northern New Jersey and New York City. Its many activities and

meetings were arranged and scheduled according to the suburban interests of its congregation. But for most of its long history, almost none of these things were true. For almost a century, from the last years of Henry Cook's ministry until the late years of James Mason's ministry, the membership was only about one-tenth its present size. It has only been very recently that there has been more than one minister. Only two of the five major boards, the Board of Trustees and the Session, could trace its history back to the establishment of a separate church. For almost all its history its congregation has come from a rural farming community; many of its parishioners in the past have been skilled artisans and laborers. And finally, for over half of its history, the Church was not even known by its present name.

Yet there are many links with the past, and the vitality and strength of the church have come from its flexibility and its adaptability to the changing conditions of the life of its times. What is the heritage of this modern suburban Protestant church? How did it come to be what it is now?

The historian is never certain about beginnings. In a sense there are none. History is a continuous and unbroken fabric; to write it means to make some judgment about where to break in to that fabric in order to establish a starting point. The history of our Presbyterian Church could begin in Metuchen, or Woodbridge; Newbury, Massachusetts, or Leith, Scotland. It could begin with the English Puritans or the Scotch Presbyterians; with the ideas of John Knox or John Calvin, or indeed at any one of a number of other points.

Much of the history of the Metuchen Church is intermingled with that of the First Presbyterian Church of Woodbridge, whose parishioners built the first meeting house in Metuchen. The Woodbridge Church had in turn been established by Puritans from Newbury, Massachusetts. The pastor of their Congregational Church was John Woodbridge, and the immigrants who came from there were the first to establish themselves in the new township. It is a good place to begin — Newbury, a Puritan village founded in 1635 on the south bank of the Merrimac River, in Essex County, Massachusetts. Its Congregational Church was the fourteenth to be founded in the Massachusetts Bay Colony.

One of the original immigrants from England was John Woodbridge, a young man in his twenties, who became a selectman and Newbury's first town clerk.[1] Subsequently he became a minister and was ordained in 1644 as the first minister of the Town of Andover. Returning to England a few years later, he came back to Newbury in 1663 and served for ten years as the pastor of its church.

During his ministry, Woodbridge and his two associates, Thomas Parker and James Noyes, became the center of a controversy over the organization and authority of the church. They challenged the congregational conception of the brethren as a whole as the source of church authority, and claimed instead that elders representative of the congregation should have powers of admittance and discipline.[2] The dispute became severe enough to lead to the calling of a special synod of the Massachusetts churches, which reaffirmed the congregational pattern and repudiated the leadership of the Newbury church.[3] But the Presbyterian idea of representative church government through elders was not foreign to the settlers who were soon to emigrate to New Jersey. It is interesting to note that some of the early ministers of this Congregational Church were regarded as Presbyterian, while some of the early ministers of our own Presbyterian Church were Congregational.

In the summer of 1665, agents of Governor Philip Carteret of New Jersey were in Newbury and other towns seeking settlers for the new colony to the south. The Governor had been appointed by the two proprietors, Lord John Berkeley and Sir George Carteret, who had been granted both title to the province and the right to govern by James, Duke of York, heir to the throne of England.[4] The immediate necessity for the colony was to encourage settlement, and New England appeared to be a fruitful prospecting ground. Willing emigrants were found at Newbury, and on May 21, 1666, articles of agreement were executed between Governor Philip Carteret on behalf of the Proprietors and John Pike, Daniel Pierce, and Abraham Toppan and their associates.[5] These articles gave permission to settle one or two plantations consisting of 40 to 100 families in the area between the Rahway River and the Raritan River. Provision was made for making land grants to settlers, for choosing magistrates and military officers, and for electing deputies to the colony's General Assembly. Land was specifically allotted for the ministry and for the building of a church.

Pierce and his associates paid eighty pounds for this vast tract of land; he subsequently sold one-third of his purchase to emigrants from New Hampshire, which became the settlement of Piscataway.[6] As settlers arrived, the land was divided, roads laid out, and the community established. In remembrance of their minister at Newbury, the settlers named their community Woodbridge, and it was chartered as a township on June 1, 1669. The charter defined the boundaries as the Arthur Cull (Kill) River on the east, Elizabethtown on the north, New Piscataway on the west, and the Raritan River on the south.

Most of the provisions of the articles of agreement were incorporated into the charter itself. In particular, freemen were empowered to choose the minister, for the support of whom all persons were to contribute. Two hundred acres of upland and meadow were set aside for the maintenance of the ministry, and 100 acres for a school, all exempt from taxes and from the Lord's rent. An important article provided that any inhabitants of different religious persuasion could maintain another ministry at their own expense.[7] Woodbridge Township was thus created as a New England town. The freemen of the corporation governed the town and supported the established ministry. Any other church that came into being would not have public support; but neither would it be publicly persecuted.

The men who came to Woodbridge were farmers, carpenters, black-smiths, coopers, masons and other skilled artisans. Among the earliest families with landholdings were:[8]

> Obadiah Ayres (Newbury), 171 acres; he married the daughter of John Pike
> John Bishop (Newbury), carpenter, 470 acres; his three sons were to become prominent citizens
> Thomas Bloomfield, carpenter, 326 acres; first of a prominent family
> William Compton, 174 acres
> Samuel Hale (Newbury), 167 acres
> Jonathan Haynes (Newbury), cooper, 97 acres
> Henry Jacques, carpenter, 368 acres
> John Pike (Newbury), 399 acres, captain of militia, ancestor of the explorer Zebulon Pike
> Daniel Pierce, blacksmith, 456 acres.

The early settlers also included families from Long Island (John Conger), New Haven, and other New England towns (Stephen Kent, Hayerhill, Massachusetts).[9] By 1672, 120 families were settled in the entire township comprising 30,000 acres.[10] Evidently the land in the western section of the township underwent considerable change in ownership. There were several 120-acre parcels along what is presently the north side of Woodbridge Avenue, some of which were subdivided. By 1715 John Compton owned 40 acres in this area, as did Israel Thornall.[11] The 120-acre parcel east of these tracts was divided equally between the two sons of Obadiah Ayres, John and Samuel. Samuel Hale's 120 acres was on the west side of Parsonage Road. John Pike had 60 acres at or near the present intersection of Main Street and Woodbridge Avenue. In 1688 it was sold to Richard Smith, Jr., who may have donated part of his land for the erection of the meeting house. Landowning families in this section of the township by 1715 probably included (besides those mentioned) Tappen, Mundy, Martin and Crowell.

Meanwhile the foundations of the meeting house were laid in 1675, and the building finally finished six years later.[12] To find a minister for the church proved to be a continuing problem with only occasional temporary solutions. As early as 1669, a committee of the town went to Newark to seek the services of Abraham Pierson, Jr., who decided to stay in Newark as assistant to his father.[13] The father had been a Congregational minister in Massachusetts and at Southampton, Long Island, before coming to Newark at the time of its original settlement.[14] Abraham, Jr., was a Harvard graduate, eventually served at Newark for over 20 years, and ultimately became one of the founders and the first president of Yale in 1701. It was his son, John, who came to Woodbridge in 1714, and was the first minister to preach in the Metuchen meeting house. Meanwhile a regular minister, John Allen, a Congregationalist, was finally secured from England in 1681. Difficulties continued for many years, however, as the congregation found its pulpit vacant more often than not, and even some of the ministers who came were not always glad to serve.[15]

Another source of migration into the colony opened up in 1685 with the arrival of the ship *Henry and Francis* from Scotland. Some of the Calvinists who had been imprisoned for their beliefs by King James petitioned the authorities for permission to come to East Jersey. Their leader was George Scot, and one of his fellow prisoners was Rev. Archibald Riddle, who later served for a few years as minister of the Woodbridge Church and for a time owned 40 acres of land along the north side of Woodbridge Avenue.[16] Scot published an appeal to all Presbyterians to accompany him, and in September, 1685 some 200 immigrants left Leith, Scotland, aboard the *Henry and Francis*. The voyage of four months proved extremely difficult, with severe hardship brought on by sickness, spoiled food, and stormy seas; about 60 of the voyagers, including Scot, died at sea. The survivors, who reached Perth Amboy just at the end of the year, were the forerunners of many Scotch and Scotch-Irish who were to come to America during the following century. Lord Neil Campbell took a group of settlers to Monmouth County and in 1692 founded the Presbyterian Church at Freehold; the grave of his grandson, John, who died in 1731, is the oldest marker existing in the old church burial ground in Metuchen. Many families from Scotland and northern Ireland were to become established in the new township: Mundaye, Payne, Kelly, Noe, Daniels, Freeman, Ross, Talmadge, Thornel, Ford.[17]

Since the immigrants from Scotland were Presbyterians, not Congregationalists, the question can be raised as to just what the early church considered itself to be. That the answer was not entirely clear to the inhabitants is suggested in a letter an early settler wrote to Scotland in 1684: "They go under the name of Independents, but are most like to Presbyterians." Another called the church service "a union of Independency, Presbyterianism, and Establishment."[18] A later historian remarked that after the Woodbridge Church joined the newly established Presbytery of Philadelphia, it was the only Presbyterian Church in which there were a number of New England men, and that fact gave the Presbytery more trouble than all the other churches put together.[19]

The Presbyterian form of Calvinism had been established in Scotland by John Knox in the 16th century, with a complete structure of Presbyteries, Synods, and General Assembly.[20] But in England, except briefly under Oliver Cromwell, the Presbyterians never succeeded in becoming the established church. There Calvinism became Puritanism, an effort to purify and reform the Anglican Church. Under continued persecution by the Stuart Kings in the 17th century, the Puritans could not achieve any permanent organization and came to rely instead on the strength of their individual congregations. Believing that the State must be governed only by the holy and regenerate, they were able to establish their idea of the union of civil and religious authority only when they migrated to Massachusetts. The New England Congregational Church not only monopolized public worship but made membership in the church a necessary qualification for voting.

The New England Puritan and the Scotch-Irish Presbyterian both looked to John Calvin as the source of their Christian beliefs, but their different historical experience led to a basic theological difference in their respective conception of what constituted the true church. To the Puritans, the covenant of the saints constituted the visible church; there was therefore no necessity for any higher organization, and no necessity for the principle of representation within the church. The brethren of any one congregation made all decisions. The Presbyterian conception of the true church lay in a broader and more general idea that encompassed a whole people; individual congregations were subordinate parts of this whole and could be represented by elders in Presbytery or Synod where decisions about the church as a whole were made. This principle of representation could be carried out within a single church too. Membership was not restricted to the saints, but encompassed all who subscribed in general to Calvinistic principles.[21] These differences sometimes became blurred in the actual practices followed by particular churches. Some Puritan congregations invited Scotch Presbyterian ministers to occupy their pulpits, but kept their congregational form of government.[22] The Woodbridge Church was an example of this since it had no active Session until late in the 18th century.

The situation in New Jersey was different from that in Scotland, or England, or New England. The original proprietors of the colony were Anglicans, but as landlords they needed settlers if their colony was to prosper. Hence the early agreements provided that no one could be persecuted for religious belief as long as there was no disturbance of the civil peace.[23] The 24 proprietors who bought East Jersey after the death of Sir George Carteret provided in their constitution in 1681:

"All persons living in the Province who confess and acknowledge the one Almighty and Eternal God, and hold themselves
obliged in conscience to live peacefully and quietly in a civil
society, shall in no way be molested or prejudged for their
religious persuasion and exercise in matters of faith and worship, nor shall they be compelled to frequent and maintain
any religious worship, place or ministry whatsoever."[24]

A permissive situation was thus created. The colony of New Jersey, unlike New England, and unlike England or Scotland, was not to have an
established church. Among the early settlements were Puritans at Elizabeth, Newark, and Woodbridge; Baptists at Middletown and Piscataway;
Quakers at Shrewsbury; Reformed at Bergen; Presbyterians at Freehold.[25]
Furthermore, even though each settlement had its one church, supported
by public taxation, the passage of time brought the founding of different
churches within the same community, and the financial support for the
ministry came to be based not on public taxation but on subscription of
the members. In Woodbridge these changes were beginning to take place
during the ministry of Samuel Shepherd in the opening years of the 18th
century.[26]

The plurality of religious organizations, the trend toward the separation of civil and religious authority, and the occasional friction that developed between the royal governors and the churches after 1702 all
created an incentive for the Congregational Churches in New Jersey to
develop a closer organization in order to maintain themselves.[27] When
the Presbytery of Philadelphia was founded in 1706 under the leadership of Francis Makemie, a Scotch Presbyterian missionary who came
to America in the 1680s,[28] the New Jersey and Long Island churches
rapidly sought admission. Woodbridge was admitted in 1710, and by
1716 the Presbytery had 40 churches claiming 3,000 members. Increasing migration of Scotch-Irish confirmed the trend toward Presbyterian
organization. In 1729 the Synod of the church (organized in 1717) adopted

as its standard of doctrinal belief the Westminster Confession of Faith of 1647, with the statement that ministers were to subscribe to its "necessary and essential articles."[29] It is this doctrinal statement which is currently being revised and made more relevant to the problems of today by a committee of the General Assembly in a process that will reach final acceptance in 1967.

The establishment of the Presbytery of Philadelphia, preceding by one year the Philadelphia Baptist Association, created the first intercolonial body among American churches. Since neither the Presbytery nor the Synod had any connection with the Presbyterian Church in Scotland, what this action did was to establish an exclusively American Church authority, completely separate from Europe, and long before this occurred in most other denominations.[30] It also established a religious authority separate from the civil power of the royal governor. It was an important step in the long and complex process of the Americanization of the Presbyterian Church. Finally, it made possible the building of a meeting house in Metuchen without fear that the inhabitants would lose their civil rights.

The minister at Woodbridge in 1707 was Nathaniel Wade, a Boston Congregationalist, whose decided opinions and imperious bearing stirred up considerable conflict within the congregation.[31] The Presbytery, hoping to alleviate the dissension and to counteract Wade's own critical views, suggested that the Presbyterian John Boyd of Freehold preach occasionally at Woodbridge, and also admitted Wade to Presbytery in 1710. The controversy continued, however, and Wade was finally ordered in 1712 to cease exercising the ministerial office.[32] Meanwhile some of Wade's opponents invited Rev. Edward Vaughan from Elizabeth in 1711, and under his leadership they seceded from the church to form an Episcopal congregation.[33] A membership list begun by Wade showed 47 members in 1708, 20 added in 1709, and 8 in 1710.[34] The three original members were Samuel Hail, John Pike, and Noah Bishop, all immigrants from Newbury, Massachusetts.

So the foundations had been laid. New Englanders had organized a community on the Congregational pattern; Scotch Presbyterians and the New Jersey environment had made the pattern Presbyterian; and in the early years of the 18th century the community was already beginning to recognize a variety of religious persuasion. The process of Americanization was under way. It was to receive a great impetus in the ministry of John Pierson.

CHAPTER VIII – FOOTNOTES

1. Joshua Coffin, *A Sketch of the History of Newbury, Newburyport, and West Newbury from 1635 to 1845*, Boston, 1845, 9-19.
2. Coffin, *op. cit.*, 39, 44, 54, 72-3; *Contributions to the Ecclesiastical History of Essex County, Massachusetts*, Boston 1865, 340; Leonard J. Trinterud, *The Forming of An American Tradition*, Philadelphia, 1949, 21.
3. Thomas J. Wertenbaker, *The Founding of American Civilization, The Middle Colonies*, New York, 1938, 170.
4. When New Jersey later became a royal colony, the proprietors gave up their right to govern but not their territorial rights. Their heirs are still occasionally active in land business; the East Jersey Proprietors are located in Perth Amboy.
5. The following provisions of the agreement were taken from the true handwritten copy in possession of the church, made from records of the State of New Jersey, January 22, 1800. The town system of settlement had been established by Governor Richard Nicolls. See Irving S. Kull, ed., *New Jersey, A History*, New York 1930, I, 96-7, 99-103.
6. Title was transferred in December, 1666. The present west boundary of Metuchen is part of the original boundary between Woodbridge and Piscataway. See *Metuchen, The Brainy Borough*, unpublished, ch. 1, p. 3-4 (hereafter referred to as Library Manuscript).

7. Copy of that part of charter dealing with religious provisions is in possession of the church. See also Earl S. Miers, *Where The Raritan Flows,* New Brunswick, New Jersey, 1964, 10-11; Irving S. Kull, ed., *New Jersey, A History,* New York 1930, I, 171.

8. W. Woodford Clayton, ed., *History of Union and Middlesex Counties, New Jersey,* Philadelphia 1882, 555-6; John P. Wall and Harold E. Pickersgill, eds., *History of Middlesex County, New Jersey,* 1664-1920, New York, 1921, I, 19; II, 402; Ezra Hunt, *Metuchen and Her History,* New York 1870, 3; Coffin, *op. cit.,* 291-322.

9. James G. Mason, *History of Metuchen,* New Brunswick, New Jersey, p. 58 mentions the Crowells and Carmans from Connecticut, and Mundy as an early resident.

10. Miers, *op. cit.,* 11. A few years later the two towns of Woodbridge and Piscataway became the nucleus of Middlesex County.

11. A detailed description of these land transactions is in Library Manuscript, *op. cit.,* 5-10.

12. This small building, 30' square, lasted well over a century. Some of its black walnut pews are still in use in the present church, at Rahway Avenue and Carteret Road in Woodbridge. New Brunswick *Sunday Home News,* June 21, 1964, section C; Rev. Joseph M. McNulty, *Historical Discourse Delivered at the Two Hundredth Anniversary of the First Presbyterian Church, Woodbridge, New Jersey, June 20, 1875,* New York, 1875, p. 5. Two other Congregational Churches, at Elizabeth and Newark, preceded the founding of Woodbridge.

13. Joseph W. Dally, *History of Woodbridge and Vicinity.*

14. Charles A. Briggs, *American Presbyterianism,* New York 1885, 100, 121; E. H. Gillette, *History of the Presbyterian Church in the U.S.A.,* Philadelphia 1864, 33, 40; G. J. Slosser, ed. *They Seek a Country — The American Presbyterians,* 1955, ch. 2, p. 30.

15. Clayton, *op. cit.,* 570; McNulty, *op. cit.,* 9; Wall and Pickersgill, *op. cit.,* 404.

16. Library manuscript, *op. cit.,* ch. 1, p. 16; Joseph H. Kler, *God's Happy Cluster — History of the Bound Brook Presbyterian Church, 1688-1963,* p. 7-8; 13. Riddle sold his land to Samuel Ayres in 1715.

17. Hunt, *Metuchen and Her History, op. cit.,* 5-6; Kull, *op. cit.,* 339-41; Wall and Pickersgill, *op. cit.,* 24; II, 371-2; Mason, *op. cit.,* 58. Bound Brook, Freehold and Basking Ridge were all settled by the Scotch-Irish.
18. *Encyclopedia of the Presbyterian Church in the U.S.A.,* 1884, p. 1039.
19. Charles Hodge, *The Constitutional History of the Presbyterian Church in the U.S.A.,* Philadelphia 1839, Part I, 87.
20. This was set forth in the Second Book of Discipline in 1577. Wertenbaker, *op. cit.,* 162-3.
21. Perry Miller, *The New England Mind,* ch. 15.
22. Clifton E. Olmstead, *Religion in America, Past and Present,* Englewood Cliffs, New Jersey 1961, 34-5.
23. Kull, *op. cit.,* 103, 321.
24. Kull, *op. cit.,* 327.
25. Kull, *op. cit.,* 108-110; 320-1.
26. Wallace N. Jamison, *Religion in New Jersey: A Brief History,* Princeton 1964, 17.
27. Trinterud, *op. cit.,* 32-3; Wertenbaker, *op. cit.,* 172-3; Jamison, *op. cit.,* 35; William Starr Myers, ed., *The Story of New Jersey,* New York 1945, II, 261.
28. Olmstead, *op. cit.,* 35. Makemie preached at Woodbridge in 1706; see Jamison, *op. cit.,* 35-6.
29. Hodge, *op. cit.,* 150 ff.; Wertenbaker, *op. cit.,* 176-7; Jamison, *op. cit.,* 37; William W. Sweet, *The Story of Religion in America,* New York 1930, 180-1.
30. Slosser, *op. cit.,* 33-4 says the Presbytery of Philadelphia preceded any other comparable body by at least 40 years. See also Olmstead, *op. cit.,* 31-2, 36.
31. McNulty, *op. cit.,* 10-11; Hodge, *op. cit.,* 83; Sweet, *op. cit.,* 178.
32. *Records of the Presbyterian Church in the U.S.A.,* Philadelphia 1841, 11-26.
33. McNulty, *op. cit.,* 10; Charles Briggs, *American Presbyterianism,* New York 1885, 159-160. Samuel Shepherd had invited the Episcopalian George Keith to preach in 1702. See Wall and Pickersgill, *op. cit.,* 407-8.
34. *A Record for Ye Church of Christ in Woodbridge beginning 1707;* Clayton, *op. cit.,* 570-1.

Chapter IX

JOHN PIERSON AND THE GREAT AWAKENING

"Mr. John Pierson having performed these points of trial assigned him, viz, preached a popular sermon from Titus, III, 8,
delivered an exegesis on that question, answered to many questions touching theological matters, and also discovered his skill
in the original languages; all which being done to satisfaction,
the said Mr. Pierson was ordained and set apart to the work of
the ministry at Woodbridge, on the 29th day of April 1717 ...
before a very great assembly."
    – *Records of the Presbyterian Church in the U.S.A.*
        (Minutes of the Presbytery of Philadelphia)

"Brethren, we were born not merely for ourselves, but the
Publick Good which as members of society we are obliged ...
to promote."

– Gilbert Tennent

JOHN PIERSON came to Woodbridge in 1714, and rapidly smoothed
over the quarrel that had erupted over Nathaniel Wade. Pierson's father,
Abraham Jr., had been pastor of the Newark Church and subsequently the
first president of Yale. John graduated from Yale in 1711, was ordained at

Woodbridge on April 29, 1717, and remained there until 1753.[1] In that span of years he was to become one of the colony's outstanding ministers, taking a leading role in Synod affairs, sympathetic to the ideas of the Great Awakening, and active in helping the church to solve the problems that the revival raised. He was instrumental in founding the College of New Jersey for the training of Presbyterian ministers, and effective in furthering the process of Americanization through his ability to relate his theological training to the conditions of colonial society. Within his congregation, he acquired a reputation of being a strict disciplinarian, and was later characterized as "sound in faith, of exemplary conversation and conduct, he well supported the dignity of his office; had but few equals in his day in theological knowledge."[2] Pierson's salary was set at eighty pounds a year, to be paid by subscription, and he had the use of the parsonage land of 200 acres.[3]

It was sometime in the early years of Pierson's ministry, between 1715 and 1730, that the first meeting house was built in Metuchen. Probably the exact date of this event will never be known. The first entry in The Session Book, Volume I states:

> "A.D. 1717. There was a small church built in the north west part of the township of Woodbridge called Metuchen for the purpose of preaching lectures in every fourth week on weekday by the Rev. Mr. John Pierson then minister of the first Presbyterian congregation in the township aforesaid to which congregation we were then united."

Since this volume begins with the minutes of Session after the separation of the two congregations in 1793, it was probably written about the time that Henry Cook became pastor, some 80 years after the event. A legal brief drawn up in 1795 in connection with the suit over the parsonage land says that the meeting house was built in Pierson's time about 70 or 80 years ago, in other words, between 1715 and 1725. A chronology prepared after 1795 by Ichabod Potter, town clerk of Woodbridge, states that the Metuchen meeting house was built about 1720 or 1730. Our anniversary is based upon the Session Book record, which may be correct, but it cannot be substantiated and it is not contradicted by any other source. Whatever the date, the meeting house, located at the junction of the Bonhamtown-Oak Tree road and the Woodbridge-Metuchen road, was rarely if ever used for church services, but rather for occasional weekday lectures or sermons for the benefit of the Woodbridge parishioners who lived in the western part of the township. By 1730 a graveyard was established by the meeting house, giving the area a more definite identification, and upon these foundations a larger meeting house was built in the 1750s. It is sometime in the latter decade that a true church may be said to have been founded.[4]

In the first half of the 18th century, because of expanding population, the absence of an established church, and the influence of the religious upheaval known as the Great Awakening, many new churches began to be founded as new centers of rural population began to develop. So the Rahway Church was founded in the 1740s by Woodbridge communicants, and Westfield split off from Elizabeth in 1727.[5] With this growth the church as a whole underwent periodic reorganization. In 1733 the Presbytery of East Jersey was created; and in 1738, six churches in East Jersey, including Woodbridge, and eight on Long Island united to form the Presbytery of New York, which was soon to become one of the Synod's leading Presbyteries.[6]

The Great Awakening of the 1730s and 1740s was an important influence leading to the establishment of new churches and the revitalization of old ones. After the first impulse of new colonization in the 17th century, a widespread indifference to the church as a moral force in colonial life set in. Frontier life was hard and unrewarding; there were no educational institutions, little social activity, frequent competition and disputes over land ownership, much callousness and little kindness. Many ministers, clinging to old ideas, did not adapt themselves or their ideas to American conditions.[7] The Revival was an appeal to the individual on the need for an active faith, the leading of a holy life, and working to realize the kingdom of God. It emphasized man's sinful nature, tried to make understandable the terror of not being a True Christian, and preached the need for repentance and regeneration by the divine Spirit. It was critical of outmoded orthodoxy and irrelevant formalism, and it deplored the moral degeneration it found everywhere.[8] Revival preaching was confined to established church services, usually Sunday morning and Sunday afternoon and one week-day afternoon, and it emphasized not immediate conversion but the need for individual struggle with conscience, aided by frequent pastoral visiting and counseling. Only by a mighty struggle within himself could sinful man know repentance and true faith.[9] Some of Gilbert Tennent's sermon titles were: The Danger of Forgetting God; The Necessity of Religious Violence; A Solemn Warning to the Secure World. It was a movement, in short, to make the role of religion a real and vital thing in the life of the individual. To the extent that it was successful, it was another important step in the Americanization of Christianity, and, in New Jersey particularly, of the Presbyterian church.

The strongest center of the revival within the Presbyterian church was in the Presbytery of New Brunswick, where three of the sons of William Tennent were all active. John Tennent and William Tennent, Jr. at Freehold, and Gilbert Tennent at New Brunswick had been in contact with Theodore Frelinghuysen in the Raritan Valley area.[10] Gilbert Tennent's sermons were designed to shake the smugness of self-satisfaction into new dedication to do God's work; in the course of their delivery he could evoke sobs and shrieks from his hearers.[11] Jonathan Dickinson at Newark was another exponent of the new way. Both Dickinson and Gilbert Tennent preached at Woodbridge, where Pierson and his congregation proved receptive to the revivalists.[12] Rev. James Mason later recorded a statement by the Thornal sisters that their grandfather sometimes brought Tennent over from New Brunswick to preach at Metuchen.

The ideas and activities of the revivalists flung a challenge at established ways that was bound to evoke controversy. At least three major issues emerged that were to cause serious division within the church. One was the fact that many of the revivalists wanted to preach in other pulpits than their own, where they could stir up the people even if their own minister was unsympathetic. An outstanding example of this itinerant preaching was set in New Jersey by George Whitefield, the great English evangelist, who came to the colonies in 1739 and on Pierson's invitation, preached in Woodbridge on April 28, 1740 to an open air congregation of about 2,000 people outside the church.[13] His powerful voice and his dramatic appeal for a new birth in Christ were to deeply influence many congregations throughout the middle colonies.

A second issue revolved around the need for liberalizing the training of candidates for the ministry, in particular the need to examine candidates as to their experimental acquaintance with religion. It was largely to meet this need that William Tennent, Sr. had founded Log College in Pennsylvania. Some of the ministers trained there were preaching in other parishes than their own.[14] This issue implied a strong criticism of many ministers with orthodox education and training, that is, that they did not fully commit themselves to their calling. Gilbert Tennent's famous sermon in 1739, The Danger of an Unconverted Ministry, charged that opponents of the revival had training and orthodoxy but were dead in heart; they were not true shepherds for their flock. A minister ought to have a divine call; "Our Lord will not make men ministers, till they follow Him."[15] Tennent's flamboyant mannerisms and raving sermons on hellfire and damnation brought him much criticism from more conservative clergymen.

A third and related issue arose over whether Presbytery or Synod was the proper judge of the qualifications of ministerial candidates. The revivalists, particularly in the Presbytery of New Brunswick, strongly emphasized the authority of the Presbytery in the licensing of preachers, being able thus to allow those whose training had been at Log College to practice the ministry.[16]

Naturally these challenges did not go unanswered. In 1737 and 1738 the Synod made two decisions to control these developments. It prohibited members of one Presbytery preaching to congregations of another without an invitation. And it decided that candidates for the ministry must have a diploma from either a European or a New England college, or apply to Synod for examination before a committee.[17] These decisions were followed by a dispute over the licensing of a member of the New Brunswick Presbytery, which led to the expulsion of that Presbytery from the Synod of Philadelphia. Other advocates of the new way eventually withdrew from the Synod and in 1745 formed the rival Synod of New York, with thirteen ministers from the Presbytery of New Brunswick, and nine from the Presbytery of New York. John Pierson played a prominent role in helping to form the new Synod; he was later to be instrumental in bringing about the reunion that occurred in 1758.[18]

As it turned out, the new Synod, representing a union of the Tennents with their Scotch Calvinist supporters, and the New England trained members of the New York Presbytery, held what was to become the prevailing view. To them, the revival was the work of God, and a minister of the word should be not only versed in doctrine but Christian in conduct. Their goal was not to transplant a European church to America, but to adapt the church that they knew to American life.[19] The two rival Synods were about equal in the number of their ministers in 1745, but by the reunion of 1758, the Synod of New York had grown from 23 to 73 ministers, and the orthodox Synod of Philadelphia had remained stationary.[20] The largest Presbytery was New York (to which Woodbridge belonged), with 23 ministers, of whom 16 were graduates of Yale, and four of the College of New Jersey. In the reunited Synod as a whole, only 15 of the 78 ministers were graduates of universities in Scotland and Ireland — another mark of the process of Americanization.

Before the reunion occurred, the Synod of New York recognized the immediate need to establish a new college for the training of ministers. The calls for ministers far exceeded the available supply, and statistics relating to the period all showed the number of vacant pulpits almost as large as the number of filled ones. Log College had not proven sufficient to fill the need. Accordingly in 1745, four prominent ministers of the Synod, all favorable to the Great Awakening, petitioned the governor of New Jersey, Lewis Morris, to found a college. The four were John Pierson, some 30 years at Woodbridge; Jonathan Dickinson, already 36 years at Elizabeth; Ebenezer Pemberton, at New York for 18 years; and Aaron Burr, at Newark for nine years.[21] Because of traditional Anglican hostility, Morris refused, but an interim governor, John Hamilton, granted a charter in 1746, and a revised one was granted in 1748 by Governor Jonathan Belcher. The College of New Jersey first met in Dickinson's parsonage in Elizabeth, then in Burr's in Newark, and finally in 1756 moved to the town of Priceton.[22] All but one of the clerical members of its Board of Trustees were members of the Synod of New York.

So it was that John Pierson, minister of the Woodbridge Church, sometime preacher at Metuchen meeting house, grandson of a Massachusetts Congregational minister, son of the Harvard trained minister of the Newark Church who was unsuccessfully sought for Woodbridge in 1669 and who later became a founder and first president of Yale, graduate of Yale, became instrumental in the founding of Princeton, and for nineteen years served on its Board of Trustees. So much has one family in one church contributed to the cause of higher education. Pierson left Woodbridge in 1753 to preach in Mendham, New Jersey, where he finally died in 1770.

By 1760, the separation from Europe was complete. The Presbyterian church had begun in the colonies under conditions lacking an established church; in its Presbyteries and Synod it had created an exclusively American authority; its outlook had been revitalized by the Great Awakening; it had founded its own educational institution to train its ministers,

71

and the great majority of its ministers were graduates of the colonial colleges. In short, well before the American Revolution, it had become an American institution.[23] Symbolically perhaps this was marked for Woodbridge by the decision of the freeholders in 1754 to appoint a committee to seek a charter for the church, in order to preserve in perpetuity the uses of the land according to the intent of the original inhabitants, i.e., the ground on which the meeting house stood, the burial ground, and the parsonage land. On September 8, 1756, a charter was granted by King George II to the First Presbyterian Church of Woodbridge.[24]

CHAPTER IX – FOOTNOTES

1. *Records of the Presbyterian Church in the U.S.A.*, Philadelphia, 1841, 43; Helen Wright, *The First Presbyterian Congregation, Mendham, Morris Co., N. J.*, Jersey City 1939, 49; Rev. Joseph M. McNulty, *Historical Discourse Delivered at the Two Hundredth Anniversary of The First Presbyterian Church, Woodbridge, N. J., June 20, 1875*, New York, 1875, 11.
2. McNulty, *op. cit.*, 11, quoting Azel Roe. See also Wright, *op. cit.*, 48.
3. S. D. Alexander, *The Presbytery of New York 1738 to 1888*, New York 1888, 4-5. A copy of a survey made of the parsonage land in 1745 shows 221 acres.
4. I have had some guidance from a copy of a letter from Henry Soskin to Viola Hutchinson, loaned to me by J. Lloyd Grimstead. The discussion of the changes in the 1750s is at the beginning of Chapter 3.
5. Thomas J. Wertenbaker, *The Founding of American Civilization: The Middle Colonies*, New York 1938, 139-142; Herbert K. England, *Historical Sketch of the Presbytery of Elizabeth*, June 1925.
6. *Records of the Presbyterian Church in the U.S.A.*, Philadelphia 1841, 104, 136-7.
7. Leonard J. Trinterud, *The Forming of An American Tradition*, Philadelphia 1949, 36-7.

8. Trinterud, *op. cit.*, 57-9, 76-9; Wertenbaker, *op. cit.*, 179; Charles Hodge, *The Constitutional History of the Presbyterian Church in the U.S.A.*, Philadelphia 1839, Part II,56-7.

9. Trinterud, *op. cit.*, 65, 177-182; William W. Sweet, *The Story of Religion in America*, New York 1930, 185. Wallace N. Jamison, *Religion in New Jersey — A Brief History*, Princeton 1964, 40.

10. Trinterud, *op. cit.*, 53; Sweet, *op. cit.*, 202-3; Clifton E. Olmstead, *Religion in America, Past and Present*, Englewood Cliffs, N. J., 1961, 41-2. Gilbert Tennent was pastor of the New Brunswick Presbyterian Church from 1726 to 1742.

11. Olmstead, *op. cit.*, 42.

12. Trinterud, *op. cit.*, 84.

13. *George Whitefield's Journals*, London, 1960, 414. Trinterud, *op. cit.*, 86; Olmstead, *op. cit.*, 42; O. B. Monnette, *First Settlers of Ye Plantations of Piscataway and Woodbridge;* Jamison, *op. cit.*, 45; Whitefield was a graduate of Oxford and an ordained priest in the Church of England.

14. Trinterud, *op. cit.*, 61-4; Sweet, *op. cit.*, 204; Gaius J. Slosser, *They Seek A Country: The American Presbyterians*, 1955, 53-6.

15. Trinterud, *op. cit.*, 89; Olmstead, *op. cit.*, 45.

16. Records of the Presbyterian Church, *op. cit.*, 145-6; Hodge, *op. cit.* Part II, 125.

17. Records, *op. cit.*, 133, 139-40; Hodge, *op. cit.* Part II, 124.

18. Trinterud, *op. cit.*, 104-120; Hodge, *op. cit.*, Part II, 179-219, 322-335. Before 1745, the Synod of Philadelphia was the highest judicatory body in the church; it was the only Synod in the colonies, since the General Assembly was not created until 1789.

19. Trinterud, *op. cit.*, 120.

20. Trinterud, *op. cit.*, 152; Sweet, *op. cit.*, 208.

21. Trinterud, *op. cit.*, 124-5.

22. Alexander, *op. cit.*, 14-15. Dickinson and Burr were its first two presidents.

23. Olmstead, *op. cit.*, 47. The revival had established significant intercolonial ties which were soon to bear fruit.

24. McNulty, *op. cit.*, 11; John P. Wall and Harold E. Pickersgill, eds., *History of Middlesex County, N. J., 1664-1920*, New York, 1921, II, 405.

Chapter X

AZEL ROE; THE ORGANIZATION OF
A SEPARATE CHURCH

"America has run off with a Presbyterian parson."
– Remark attributed to Horace Walpole

"We cannot help congratulating you on the general and almost universal attachment of the Presbyterian body, to the cause
of liberty and the rights of mankind ... The Synod, therefore,
request you to render thanks to Almighty God, for all his mercies spiritual and temporal; and in a particular manner for establishing the independence of the United States of America."
– Synod Letter of 1783

"The consideration of the petition of Woodbridge was resumed
and after a most serious deliberation — it was [decided] that
the Prayer of the petition of Woodbridge be granted and that
the Union between Woodbridge and Metuching be dissolved...."
– Minutes of the Presbytery of New York, May 9, 1793

ABOUT THE TIME that John Pierson left, a larger meeting house was
built on the site of the old burial ground. In Hunt's History the building is
described as being about 36 feet by 25 feet, enclosed with shingles; the

75

four-sided roof had no steeple. The center aisle ran in an east-west direction, leading to a high pulpit at the east end; there were two parallel side aisles. In front and to the left of the pulpit was a place for the clerk of the singing. An aisle along the front of the pulpit led out the front door on the south side. The floor plan of June 2, 1784, shows 42 pews, plus 22 more seats in the gallery, reached by a stairway in the rear.[1] The floor may have been covered with sand, and the only heat in winter came from foot-warmers brought by the parishioners.[2] At the time that this church was built the people applied for part of the preaching on the Sabbath, but this request was refused.[3]

The church in Woodbridge, meanwhile, was temporarily supplied by Timothy Allen, a Congregationalist minister, and after 1755 by Nathaniel Whittaker, a graduate of the College of New Jersey.[4]

It was probably during Whittaker's ministry, in 1755 or 1756, that the Metuchen congregation decided to incorporate and unite with the Presbytery of New Brunswick. Again we cannot be sure about the date. In his later chronology, Ichabod Potter listed 1755. Azel Roe, writing about 50 years after the event, also said 1755. The Session Book record later compiled by Henry Cook said 1756. Alexander's History of the Presbytery of New York indicated shortly after 1755. On the 200th anniversary of the Woodbridge church in 1875, Rev. McNulty said the separate church at Metuchen was first established in Whittaker's ministry; 50 years later, on the 250th anniversary, Rev. Buschman said in the late 1750s. The various histories of Middlesex County do not shed any further light on the problem.[5] Dr. James Mason, contrary to most other sources, thinks the separation occurred in 1760, citing local dissensions in the church, the fact that the church was located at a central point for the farmers in that part of the township, and the interruptions in church attendance as a result of a smallpox epidemic in that year.[6] This date is also mentioned in a history of the Presbytery of Elizabeth, which states that the Great Awakening brought into existence eight new churches, one of which was the Metuchen Church.[7]

Whatever the correct date for the first founding of a separate church, most likely 1755 or 1756, the first pastor at Metuchen may have been Alexander Cummings, who had been born in Freehold and ordained at New York in 1750. He left in 1761 to accept a call to the Congregationalist Old South Church in Boston.[8] For about the next nine years, continued temporary supply came from a number of different preachers of the New Brunswick Presbytery, but none accepted a permanent call to the church.[9] This unsatisfactory experience was probably one reason that impelled Metuchen to seek to rejoin Woodbridge about 1770. Another reason was that a continued separate existence would voluntarily forfeit any claim to share in the parsonage land.[10] Though again the exact date is uncertain, it was probably in 1770 that the two congregations were re-united, and preaching occurred at Metuchen on a more regular basis.

These difficulties were by no means unusual. During the frontier expansion of the 18th century, it proved extremely difficult for the Synod to find qualified ministers for the churches that sprang up faster than they could be staffed. Quite frequently established ministers from older congregations were asked to spend a month or two on the frontier, with Synod furnishing a temporary supply to their regular church. In 1770, for instance, Azel Roe was ordered by Synod to go to Virginia and the Carolinas to preach the gospel, ordain elders and administer the sacrament; the Presbytery of New York was directed to supply his pulpit during his absence.[11] It was fortunate for a church to be able to have one pastor over an extended period of time.

Farming was the chief activity of the people of Middlesex County before the Revolution. Winter wheat was the chief cash crop, and corn, rye, barley and oats were also grown. Cattle raising was increasingly important; cabbages were grown, peaches and apples cultivated. New York was a major market for agricultural produce shipped through New Brunswick and Perth Amboy. Flour, bread, corn, lumber, beef, cabbages all were exported to New York.[12] Weekly markets were held at Perth

Amboy, and Woodbridge and other communities had two-day fairs in May and in October for trading purposes.[13] Court day at Perth Amboy brought crowds to the inns for meals and lodging, and to see some of the aristocracy of the colony.[14] Many of the products used in everyday life were made on the farm itself. Women spun yarn, smoke-cured meat, brewed beer, peach brandy and apple cider, and made candles and soap. Rural social events were built around these activities; there were apple paring bees, quilting bees, and wood frolics to supply the minister with firewood.[15] The church was the most important institution to bring people together.

In 1763, Azel Roe, the famous rebel clergyman of New Jersey, came to Woodbridge as its minister, a post he was to hold for 52 years until his death in 1815 at the age of 77. A Long Islander by birth, he graduated from the College of New Jersey in 1756 at the age of 18, was ordained to the ministry a few years later, and in 1800 received a Doctor of Divinity degree from Yale. He began to preach part time in Metuchen in 1770, and after 1772 he preached half time in each of his congregations.[16] In theory it was still only one church, however, since one Session served both. Rev. Joseph McNulty later characterized the relationship as one church in matters of government and discipline, separate and distinct in temporalities, sharing equally in the services of the minister.[17] This union lasted 23 years until its permanent dissolution in 1793. As a minister, Roe's manners were graceful and dignified; his preaching was "distinguished by substantial excellence, rather than those qualities which attract the multitude."[18] McNulty described Roe as energetic and zealous, of commanding presence, a devoted patriot who took an active part in supporting the cause of independence from Great Britain.[19] A personal incident is recorded in which a Mrs. Campbell reminded her husband, on one of Roe's pastoral visits, "Dugall, don't you know that Parson Roe is to preach here tonight, and we have not a drop of spirits in the house." A messenger was sent to Bricktown (Rahway) to remedy the deficiency.[20]

Presbyterians, both clergy and laymen, were active opponents to British colonial policy in the 1760s and 1770s. The repeal of the Stamp Act in 1766 brought an approving pastoral letter from Synod which considered the repeal a "confirmation of our liberties."[21] The Woodbridge Committee of Correspondence established in the 1770s numbered among its 21 members Henry Freeman, James Manning, John Ross, Timothy Bloomfield and John Noe, all of whom are listed in the pew rent lists of the 1780s as belonging to the Metuchen congregation.[22] In May 1775, the Synod called on its congregations to observe a day of fasting, humiliation and prayer, appointing the last Thursday of June for such observance, unless "that august body," the Continental Congress, should appoint a different one.[23] On May 22 a pastoral letter signed by the moderator stated that the people of the whole continent seemed determined to defend their rights; it warned that those who had taken up arms in the cause of liberty must be prepared for death, for war would come if Britain continued to enforce its claims by violence. The people were advised to express their attachment to King George III, emphasizing that they wanted only the preservation of their rights as freemen and as Britons. The people were urged to pray for God's direction of the proceedings of the Continental Congress, and adhere firmly to its resolutions.[24]

The struggle for the preservation of their rights against what they regarded as tyranny was a cause with which Presbyterians and their Congregational brethren had long identified themselves, both in Scotland and in England. They feared, in addition, that Parliament might try to create an American episcopate as a step toward the establishment of the Anglican Church, and they saw resistance to Parliament as partly a crusade to preserve religious freedom.[25] What made these ideas influential was the fact that Presbyterian clergymen were usually regarded as leaders in their communities. They were the most highly educated, they commanded widespread respect, and their pulpits provided excellent opportunity to mold public opinion through sermons that were frequently published and circulated among a wide audience.[26] It is little wonder that a British official was said to have remarked in 1776, "Presbyterianism is really at the Bottom of this whole Conspiracy."[27]

Azel Roe was among those ministers who stood clearly and prominently in defense of freedom and ultimately in favor of independence.[28] He contributed not only his voice but his courage as well. He took part with some of his congregation in assisting troops to resist a British attack at Blazing Star Landing, and subsequently was taken prisoner by the British and sent to Sugar House Prison in New York.[29]

Such leadership helps to account for the fact that more than half of the New Jersey troops in the Continental Army were Scotch-Irish Presbyterians. On the other hand the frequent battles in New Jersey convinced many residents to avoid supporting the cause of independence.[30] George Washington himself recorded his disappointment that so many Jerseymen refused to aid the colonial cause and took advantage of British offers of protection.[31] For some it must have been simply a matter of preservation. For a time five British regiments belonging to General Howe's Army were stationed at Bonhamtown, instilling sufficient fear in the inhabitants to make many of them actively help the British with supplies, food and information; no one could be sure how the conflict was going to turn out.[32] The British, of course, helped themselves as well. The home of Moses Bloomfield was plundered five times, losing cattle and horses, clothing and silver. Ezekiel Bloomfield suffered extensive damage to his home and fields. Many other farmers of the township not only cooperated with the colonial militia but also joined the troops to actively fight for the cause. Probably a number of skirmishes were fought in the Metuchen area, at least one causing some minor damage to the meeting house. The most important military event occurred in 1777. On June 26 a column of British troops under General Vaughan was dispatched from Staten Island via Fords and Metuchen to the area of Oak Tree; a parallel column under General Cornwallis moved to the same vicinity via

Woodbridge and Iselin. During the next day a number of clashes took place, the most severe being at Short Hills, and in the vicinity of Scotch Plains, before the British were forced to retreat via Rahway to Staten Island. The whole effort, aimed at luring Washington out of the Watchung Hills and giving Howe a chance to move across New Jersey in the direction of Philadelphia, failed, and Howe shortly embarked his army on transports to attack Philadelphia from the mouth of the Delaware River.[33]

The Metuchen congregation contributed many veterans who enlisted in Washington's army. Nineteen of the 42 pewholders of 1784 were veterans. An examination of the pewholders in the next ten years shows an additional 17 veterans — a total of 36 altogether. The Ayers family and the Mundy family contributed five each, and the Freeman family three.[34] Twenty-four of the 36 are buried in the old burial ground. All apparently were enlisted men in the army, except for Matthew Freeman and Robert Ross, both of whom were captains, and Melanthon Freeman, who was a surgeon. Twelve of the 36 are on the original membership list of the Church in 1794.

Peace came in 1783 with a treaty recognizing the independence of the United States. The Synod circulated a letter congratulating its members on their "almost universal attachment ... to the cause of liberty and the rights of mankind ... The Synod, therefore, request you to render thanks to Almighty God, for all his mercies spiritual and temporal; and in a particular manner for establishing the independence of the United States of America."[35]

The impact of these great events had made inadequate the organization of the hierarchy of the church. Attendance at Synod meetings declined during the 1780s; sometimes whole Presbyteries were unrepresented.[36] Some effort at reorganization was clearly called for. A Synod committee under the chairmanship of John Witherspoon was appointed in 1785 to draw up a plan of reorganization. The resulting plan called for the creation of a General Assembly, with four Synods and sixteen

Presbyteries.[37] The plan was approved and the first meeting of the General Assembly opened in Philadelphia on May 21, 1789, just three weeks after George Washington had taken the presidential oath. Azel Roe was a delegate to the first General Assembly; in 1802 he achieved the distinction of being chosen Moderator of the 14th General Assembly. The Presbytery of New York, to which First Church of Woodbridge and its Metuchen congregation continued to belong, was the second largest Presbytery in the church, with a total of 39 congregations.[38]

The decade of the 1780s brought the first important steps in the separation of the "upper congregation" from Woodbridge. On June 2, 1784, the first recorded meeting of the Metuchen congregation was held. Benjamin Manning was chosen clerk of the congregation, a post to which he was reelected each year until 1800. George Kelley, Ephraim Morris and Thomas Manning were designated collectors of pew rent, which was to be paid to Mr. Roe. The congregation was responsible for seventy pounds annually, which was half of the minister's salary. Anyone delinquent on pew rents was supposed to give a note for the amount to the collector, which was to be payable on demand by the minister. That first meeting also chose Matthew Freeman and Ellis Bloomfield as a committee to settle with the lower congregation, and Daniel Hampton as doorkeeper.[39] Congregation meetings were held annually, usually in April or May, for the purpose of assigning pews for the following year, and appointing the clerk, collectors, doorkeeper and other necessary officers. In 1791, for instance, the congregation appointed Capt. Matthew Freeman to be in charge of a group to collect firewood for Mr. Roe; Freeman was also to provide food and drink for those who came.

A most important meeting of the congregation occurred on April 5, 1787 when seven trustees were chosen to transact the temporal concerns of the church. The seven were Benjamin Manning, John Conger, John Ross, Ebenezer Ford, Ellis Ayres, Timothy Bloomfield and Robert Ross. At their first meeting on October 6, 1787, the Trustees, pursuant to an

Act of the New Jersey State Legislature in 1786 authorizing the incorporation of religious bodies, took the name of the Second Presbyterian Church of Woodbridge, which remained its official name for the next 70 years. Benjamin Manning was elected president, and served in that capacity until 1799.[40] Only two other meetings were held before 1792, but in that year seven meetings occurred, and also three congregational meetings, to carry out the enlargement of the church and to provide for the separation of the two congregations. During this interval there was still only one session for the two churches. In 1788, three of the six elders were from Metuchen: Matthew Freeman, Ellis Bloomfield and Melanthon Freeman.[41]

On March 1, 1792, the congregation voted to enlarge the meeting house by twenty feet.[42] The Trustees ordered James Manning to fence the burial ground with white oak posts and chestnut or cedar rails. In April they asked Woodbridge for timber from the parsonage land in order to carry out the enlargement.[43] The Woodbridge Trustees, not wishing to recognize that Metuchen had any claim to the parsonage land, countered with the suggestion that the two churches apply to Presbytery for an assistant minister. The Trustees of Second Church resolved not to join in such a request and decided to go ahead with a fifteen-foot addition to the meeting house. A committee was appointed to seek bids and to supervise the project. In May the bid of Jonathan Freeman was accepted; he expected to employ two others with an apprentice, and "asks no Rum or any other spirits." The congregation subscribed about two-hundred and seventy pounds for the enlargement, which was well under the cost of three-hundred and ninety pounds. The addition was finished in November 1792, enlarging the church to dimensions of 36 by 40 feet, increasing the pews on the main floor from 42 to 56, modifying the roof to provide a chimney, and providing a new main entrance on the east. Rents were assigned for 56 pews at a congregation meeting November 21, 1792.[44] The rents for the 42 pews in the years 1790-2 had totalled sixty pounds, eleven shillings; the 56 pews rented for ninety-two pounds, ten shillings in 1792, and for one-hundred twenty-seven pounds, six shillings for the next two years.

Meanwhile in October, the Trustees appointed Doctor Melanthon Freeman and Benjamin Manning to attend Presbytery to oppose the lower congregation's petition for a disunion.[45] The Second Church did not want a complete separation without assurance of taking over a share of the parsonage land, to which First Church claimed full title. First Church, in turn, had no intention of sharing the expense of enlarging the meeting house, which would benefit only Second Church. Therefore in the spring of 1793 Woodbridge applied for dissolution, with Metuchen to receive one-third of the preaching and one-third of parsonage rents on a year-to-year basis.[46] The Metuchen congregation voted not to support the application, and chose a committee to follow up on the matter. Finally on May 9, 1793, the Presbytery of New York acceded to Woodbridge's request and authorized the separation. It recommended the settlement as suggested by Woodbridge, urging Metuchen to accept it "until Divine Providence shall grant a better provision for them."[47] The Metuchen congregation, meeting a week later, first voted not to agree to the recommendation; then voted to agree provided that Woodbridge would give one-third of the parsonage land to Metuchen. This provision was not met, and the separation took place without agreement about the parsonage. Only later, in 1795, did the Trustees decide to institute legal proceedings to secure a share in the parsonage. Meanwhile in November of 1793 the congregation drew up a subscription to raise money to buy a parsonage of its own.

It seems difficult in retrospect to fully justify the Metuchen congregation's point of view. After all, it had been incorporated as a separate church, with a separate Board of Trustees some six years before. It was about to acquire a separate Session and its own minister. One could hardly be separate and at the same time enjoy the fruits of union. The first step in establishing a separate Session took place on April 15, 1793, when the congregation elected James Manning a ruling elder.[48] One year later, on April 22, 1794, the congregation directed the Trustees to apply to the Presbytery of New York to put a call for Mr. Henry Cook, of Mendham, New Jersey, to be settled at Metuchen. Cook accepted the call as of May 1, at a salary of one-hundred and twenty pounds, and was ordained and installed on October 14, 1794, as the first full-time minister of the Second Presbyterian Church of Woodbridge.[49]

CHAPTER X – FOOTNOTES

1. Ezra Hunt, *History of the Churches of Metuchen,* New York 1870, 2-3; William H. Ayers, *A History of the First Presbyterian Church of Metuchen, New Jersey,* Metuchen, New Jersey 1947, 12. Mr. Roe's family had the pew immediately to the right of the pulpit.
2. Ayers, *op. cit.,* 12, quoting an address of Charles C. Campbell, Superintendent of the Sunday School, in 1916.
3. Session Book, Vol. I.
4. S. D. Alexander, *The Presbytery of New York,* 1738-1888, 16-17; L. V. Buschman, *250th Anniversary of the First Presbyterian Church in Woodbridge, 1675-1925.*
5. Again I am indebted for some guidance from a copy of a letter from Henry Soskin to Viola Hutchinson, loaned to me by J. Lloyd Grimstead.
6. Rev. J. G. Mason, *The History of Metuchen, New Jersey,* New Brunswick, New Jersey, undated, 59-60. He called Whittaker "young, zealous, impulsive, brilliant, erratic."
7. Herbert K. England, *Historical Sketch of the Presbytery of Elizabeth,* June 1925.
8. Frederick L. Weis, *The Colonial Clergy of the Middle Colonies,* 1628-1776, Worcester, Massachusetts, 1957, 202. Timothy Allen of the New Brunswick Presbytery may have preached at Metuchen.
9. William Tennent, Jr. may have been among those who refused a call. Mason, *op. cit.,* 62.

10. *Metuchen, The Brainy Borough,* unpublished, ch. 11, p. 2-4 (hereafter referred to as Library Manuscript).

11. Leonard J. Trinterud, *The Forming of an American Tradition,* Philadelphia 1949, 196-8; *Records of the Presbyterian Church in the U.S.A.,* Philadelphia 1841, 404; Charles Hodge, T*he Constitutional History of the Presbyterian Church in the U.S.A.,* Philadelphia 1839, Part II, 354.

12. Thomas Wertenbaker, *The Founding of American Civilization: The Middle Colonies,* 146; Irving S. Kull, ed., *New Jersey, a History,* New York 1930, I, 275-295.

13. Kull, *op. cit.,* 292.

14. New Brunswick *Sunday Home News,* June 21, 1964, Section C.

15. *Ibid.*

16. Rev. Joseph M. McNulty, *Historical Discourse Delivered at the Two Hundredth Anniversary of the First Presbyterian Church, Woodbridge, New Jersey, June 20, 1875,* New York 1875, 12-13; Weis, *op. cit.,* 300. Roe served on the Board of Trustees of the College of New Jersey for almost thirty years.

17. McNulty, *op. cit.,* 12.

18. McNulty, *op. cit.,* 14; *Encyclopedia of the Presbyterian Church in the U.S.A.,* 1884, p. 382.

19. McNulty, *op. cit.,* 14.

20. New Brunswick *Home News,* June 15, 1917, reprinting chapter two of Mundy's History.

21. Hodge, *op. cit.,* II, 485.

22. Book of the Proceedings of the Congregation; Kull, *op. cit.,* I, 421-3; John P. Wall and Harold E. Pickersgill, eds., *History of Middlesex County, New Jersey 1664-1920,* New York 1921, I, 87.

23. Records, *op. cit.,* 465.

24. Records, *op. cit.,* 466-9; Hodge, *op. cit.,* 11,487 ff.; Trinterud, *op. cit.,* 246-8.

25. Trinterud, *op. cit.,* 236-8; William W. Sweet, *The Story of Religion in America,* New York 1930, 253.

26. *Clifton E. Olmstead, Religion in America, Past and Present,* Englewood Cliffs 1961, 50. The publication and circulation of sermons was one of the legacies of the Great Revival.

27. Trinterud, *op. cit.*, 250. Wallace N. Jamison, *Religion in New Jersey: A Brief History,* Princeton 1964, 57-8.
28. It is a well known fact that the only clergyman to sign the Declaration of Independence was John Witherspoon, a Presbyterian.
29. McNulty, *op. cit.*, 14.
30. Jamison, *op. cit.*, 58.
31. Samuel E. Morison, *The Oxford History of the American People,* New York, 1965, 241.
32. W. Woodford Clayton, ed., *History of Union and Middlesex Counties,* Philadelphia 1882, 478.
33. This account of the engagement was taken from the Plainfleld *Courier News,* April 28, 1964. The Short Hills lie along Woodland Avenue north of Oak Tree road. The damage to the church was recorded by Ezra Hunt in his later history; see in miscellaneous notes of J. Lloyd Grimstead.
34. This information comes from an analysis of the pew rent lists for the years 1784-1794. The total of 36 represents about one-third of the total number of different names on these lists for this period. See also Clayton, *op. cit.*, 478-487; *Record of Graves in Colonial Cemetery, Metuchen, New Jersey,* compiled by F. J. Sortore in 1931-2 for the Matoschoning Chapter, Daughters of the American Revolution.
35. Hodge, *op. cit.*, II, 495-6. John Witherspoon was a member of the Synod Committee that prepared the letter.
36. Trinterud, *op. cit.*, 280-1.
37. Records, *op. cit.*, 481 ff.; Hodge, *op. cit.*, Part II, 505-6; Olmstead, *op. cit.*, 58.
38. This National Presbyterian organization was preceded by the organization of the Methodist Episcopal Church in 1784. See Jamison, *op. cit.*, 74-5.
39. Book of Proceedings of the Congregation of the upper part of Woodbridge commonly called Metuching, June 2, 1784. The book includes a floor plan of the church as previously described.
40. Book of Proceedings of the Trustees of the Second Presbyterian Church of Woodbridge (pages unnumbered).
41. Minutes of Session of First Presbyterian Church of Woodbridge.
42. Book of Proceedings of the Congregation.

---

43. Book of Proceedings of the Trustees.
44. Book of Proceedings of the Congregation; Library Manuscript, *op. cit.*, ch. 11, p. 3.
45. Book of Proceedings of Trustees; McNulty, *op. cit.*, 13.
46. Book of Proceedings of the Congregation.
47. Congregation meeting of May 16, 1793, quoting minutes of the Presbytery of New York.
48. Book of Proceedings of the Congregation; Manning was a deacon in First Church. The first Session meeting did not occur until 1795.
49. Book of Proceedings of the Trustees; Alexander, *op. cit.*, 27; Helen Wright, *The First Presbyterian Congregation, Mendham, Morris County, New Jersey,* Jersey City 1939. James Pierson went to Mendham in 1753 and preached there ten years. Cook was 35 years old at the time of his call and hence could not have known Pierson.

Chapter XI

THE PASTORATE OF HENRY COOK
1794-1824

"We the Trustees of the 2nd Presbyterian Church of Woodbridge being on sufficient grounds well satisfied of the ministerial qualifications of you, Mr. Henry Cook, and having good hopes from our past experience of your labours, that your ministrations in the Gospel will be profitable to our Spiritual interests, do earnestly call and desire you to undertake the pastoral office in said congregation, promising you in the discharge of your duty all proper support, encouragement, and obedience in the Lord."

> *Book of Proceedings of the Trustees, April 29, 1794*

"He was a man of unassuming manners and of good and cultivated mind, a sound divine, a faithful and useful preacher and pastor and Christian indeed in whom there was no guile. The bereaved congregation in token of their affection have erected this stone in his memory."

> *Inscription on Henry Cook's grave in old burial ground*

HENRY COOK was not only the first but also one of the most important ministers the Metuchen Church has had. Taking over a small rural church at the beginning of its independent existence, he led it patiently and faithfully through its early organizational and financial difficulties, frequently at considerable personal sacrifice; not until after the first decade of his pastorate did it seem certain that the church would survive. Over the following two decades the church became fully established, and by the end of his pastorate in 1824 the original membership of 70 had almost tripled, to a new total of 202.[1] That total was not to go substantially and permanently beyond 200 for over 40 years after Cook's death. A graduate of Rutgers in 1789, and a member of the Presbyterian Church of Mendham, in Morris County, he was called to the Metuchen Church in 1794 and remained its pastor for 30 years, longer than any subsequent pastor except Rev. James Mason. His first wife died in 1816 and he subsequently remarried. He has been characterized as a faithful pastor, an earnest preacher, and a modest, kind-hearted individual. His scholarly attainments were fully recognized when the Presbytery of New York designated him as the only minister in the Presbytery qualified to examine candidates for the ministry in their knowledge of Hebrew.[2]

In the mid-1790s, major handicaps existed which would have to be overcome before the little church could begin to grow and to become influential in the life of the community. One handicap was the rural nature of the area. The meeting house and its surrounding farms had to compete against other and increasingly more important centers of activity. Township headquarters were in Woodbridge; the main travel road ran through Bonhamtown; the farmer's trading center was in Oak Tree.[3] There was less to attract people to the vicinity of the church, and the church no longer monopolized community activity as it once had. Secondly, the enthusiastic dedication of the whole church to the cause of revolution, and the zeal engendered by the Great Awakening had both worn themselves out. Religious feeling was declining, and many clergymen withdrew from public office. The College of New Jersey was supplying fewer candidates for the ministry in the years after the war than before.[4] The General Assembly of 1798 complained of impiety, contempt for religion, and the destruction of morals.

> "We perceive with pain and fearful apprehension a general dereliction of religious principles and practice among our fellow citizens, a visible and prevailing impiety and contempt for the laws and institutions of religion.... Profaneness, pride, luxury, injustice, intemperance, lewdness, and every species of debauchery and loose indulgence greatly abound."[5]

This climate of the times was reflected in the relative inactivity of the newly organized Session of the Church. The first meeting of the Session occurred on Saturday, June 27, 1795, at the home of James Manning, the elder who had been chosen two years earlier. The other four elders were Matthew Freeman, Melanthon Freeman, William Manning and Eliseus Bloomfield;[6] the latter two were absent from the meeting. Over the next four years, the Session met only five times, and its total business in those five years was the admission of eleven new members, and the infliction of disciplinary punishment on four members.[7] Between 1799 and 1802 it apparently did not meet officially at all. The Session was not yet the governing body of the church that it was in time to become.

In these early days, financial hardships were a permanent condition. Pew rents were frequently in arrears, and the pastor's salary depended directly upon these collections. The 56 pews rented for about one hundred and twenty-seven pounds annually, barely enough to cover Cook's salary of one hundred and twenty pounds ($600). That collections did not measure up to expectations is shown by the fact that Cook received salary due May 1, 1797, on March 31, 1798. The earlier expense of enlarging the meeting house was still being met, and in 1795 the Trustees purchased a house and lot for two hundred pounds for a parsonage, providing additional money to fence the parsonage lot and to enclose the burial ground.[8] All such expenses were paid for through special subscriptions; that providing for the purchase of the parsonage totalled three hundred and eighty-two pounds.[9] This subscription list was drawn up November 14, 1793, and provided for payment in three installments, as of May 1 in 1794, 1795, and 1796. Forty-three members subscribed, with contributions ranging from one pound five shillings to forty pounds, almost half the subscriptions being two or three pounds. William Manning, Melanthon Freeman, Matthew Freeman and James Manning together contributed about one-third of the total amount.

Financial difficulties were compounded by the legal action instituted by the Board of Trustees in 1795 to gain a favorable settlement of the dispute with the Woodbridge Church over rights to the parsonage land.[10] An effort was first made to solve this problem through negotiation. A letter from the Trustees claimed a just share in the parsonage by right and equity, and suggested the appointment of committees from each Board to discuss the matter. Woodbridge acceded to the request, though its Board stated, "... we beg leave to differ from you Intirely." The Trustees' committee, consisting of Mr. Foord, Dr. Freeman and Major Ross, was instructed to ask for one-half of the parsonage, but to accept one-third if necessary. In the course of negotiations, the Woodbridge Trustees suggested the possibility of a money payment, but when the Metuchen committee asked for seven hundred pounds, the suggestion was refused. The Metuchen Trustees thereupon determined to sue.

The first subscription to carry on the law suit totaled one hundred and thirty pounds, eight shillings and six pence. In September 1795, three attorneys were hired, Frederick Frelinghuysen, Andrew Kirkpatrick and Samuel Leake. The case was originally decided by the Court of Chancery in favor of Woodbridge, and carried by Metuchen to the Court of Appeals. On May 25, 1801, the decree of the Chancellor was upheld and the appeal dismissed. The expenses of this litigation caused the sale of the parsonage in 1803, and eventually a need to borrow money to make up the arrears in the pastor's salary.[11] Significantly, the final result of the law suit was to sever the last tie between the two congregations.[12] Equally important, the need for legal documentation produced important source material for future historians about the early history of the two churches.

The opening years of the 19th century brought considerable improvement in the fortunes of the church. Nationally, a great religious revival movement became active and spread rapidly, especially in the frontier areas of Kentucky, Tennessee, Ohio, and western New York and Pennsylvania. Open-air camp meetings, long sermons exhorting people to repent of their sins, shouting participants professing their conversion with emotional fervor — all helped to foster the frontier spirit of democratic equality. The frontier efforts of Presbyterian clergymen were important in founding new churches, but the Presbyterian insistence on a properly educated ministry and a tendency to repudiate the emotional excesses of revivalism were handicaps to the role of evangelistic leadership. Instead the frontier brought into prominence the Baptist preacher and the Methodist circuit rider.[13]

The older part of the country did not escape the influence of revivalism, though it took a somewhat different form. A religious awakening occurred under Timothy Dwight at Yale, but the increased religious zeal of the times tended to emphasize corporate activity and organization rather than individual conversion, and national and interdenominational cooperation as a proper means to the end of reemphasizing the importance of religion. Out of it came the American Board of Commissioners for Foreign Missions, the American Bible Society, and the American Sunday School Union, all established during the first quarter of the 19th century.[14] Out of it came also the founding of Princeton Theological Seminary in 1812, as training for the ministry ceased to be the major concern of the College of New Jersey.

Both the spiritual revival with its concern for individual salvation, and the expansion in organizational activity influenced the years of the

Cook ministry in the Metuchen Church. On October 15, 1803, 22 new members were received into the church, and by the end of the year 10 more had joined. The next year, 1804, 31 new members were admitted, 14 on May 5. By 1806, the church, with 132 communicants, had nearly doubled its original membership.[15]

Besides admitting new members, the chief activity of Session in these years was to oversee in strict fashion the behavior of individuals, and to inflict disciplinary punishment when appropriate. A committee of Session visited Levi Mundy because of his habit of "neglecting to attend the public worship of God." He was subsequently asked to appear before Session, where he acknowledged that he had broken the Sabbath "by going fishing on the Lord's Day." He also confessed to be intemperate in drinking. The Session suspended him from the sacraments of the church for six months.[16] A woman found herself under the Session's surveillance because her "behavior and conversation were reported to be unfriendly towards her neighbors."[17] Another woman reported to be guilty of the "sin of antenuptial fornication" had to appear before Session to confess her sin and seek forgiveness before she could be restored to the communion of the church.[18] Until well toward the middle of the 19th century, most of these confessions by individuals and subsequent discipline by Session were read publicly from the pulpit. The following quotation, from the Session minutes of November 3, 1804, provides a typical situation:

> "The Session being informed that Mr. Daniel Compton who has been for some years in a State of Suspension from the Privileges of this Church, was earnestly desirous to obtain a restoration to his former privileges — appointed Mr. Cook to visit him on some day before the day of preparation for the Communion next ensuing — and to receive in writing such confession of his sins as he shall be willing to make and present

it to the Session at their Next Meeting — which confession if
it shall be deemed satisfactory shall be read in the presence of
the congregation — after which he may be again received into
the fellowship of his Brethren."

Who informed Session of the various infractions of the people's behavior is not recorded; but clearly, the individual's private life was likely to be subject to critical public inspection at any time by a duly constituted religious authority. Nothing could better illustrate the strong role that the church played in the life of the individual.

The organizational influence of the religious life of the times on Metuchen was expressed in the founding of the Sunday School. In October, 1809, the Presbytery of New York inquired whether proper pastoral care was being exercised to teach baptized children the principles of religion. The Session resolved in 1810 to "consider it their duty to exercise a Special care over the religious instruction of all baptized children ..." They resolved also "to exercise the discipline of the Church toward those parents who having dedicated their children to God in baptism, shall be found habitually negligent in fulfilling their covenant obligations ..."[19] Again in 1815 the Presbytery asked its Sessions to make sure that baptized children understood their proper relationship to the Church of Christ, and recommended annual visits by Session to baptized persons who were not yet in full communion with the Church.[20] The result of this concern was the establishment of a Sunday School in 1816, with Robert Ross as the first superintendent. The Franklin School, built in 1807, probably housed the Sunday School for many years.[21]

The climax of revivalism for Metuchen came in 1818. For some years before that, the Session had been examining prospective members on their "knowledge of the truth and experimental acquaintance with religion." The Great Revival of 1818 brought in 118 new members, many of them having gone through the personal experience of conversion. Eighty communicants were admitted at one meeting of the Session, April 8, 1818, and at the subsequent Sabbath, April 12, 1818, 90 new members were accepted, which may be the largest number of persons ever admitted to the church at one time.[22] One of the converts, Joel Campbell, who later became a Presbyterian minister, wrote of the great event, "Some aged people were brought in - one over a hundred years of age. The people would walk two, three, and even four miles to attend a prayer meeting."[23] Apparently the revival affected a large area because other churches experienced a significant increase in membership about the same time. The membership total of 202 at the end of Cook's pastorate indicated that most of those who joined remained. Two subsequent elders, Samuel Bloodgood and Melanthon Mundy, were among the converts. Meanwhile the revival itself died out as quickly as it had flared; only 16 new members joined in the next six years.

By the second decade of the 19th century, the Second Presbyterian Church of Woodbridge had acquired a solid foundation. Increasing membership and the growing economic activity of the area meant more income to the church; annual pew rents began to be raised gradually. In 1805, the 56 pews rented for one hundred and sixty-two pounds; in 1806, $368.75 (this was the first year in which the use of dollars replaced pounds in the financial records); in 1818, $518.75; in 1824, $422.12. Pews renting annually for five or six dollars before 1818 were going for $7.50 or more after that year. The maximum of $16 advanced to $21.[24] In 1818 and 1819, small rents were listed for seats in the gallery. In 1805, Cook's salary was raised from $300 to $400, and in 1807 the Trustees purchased a lot in addition to the parsonage, and added one-third of an acre to the burying ground.[25]

In an effort to give proper leadership to hymn singing in the services, the congregation began in 1808 to appoint a chorister, or clerk for singing. By 1814 there were two choristers and an assistant to help in "raising the psalms."[26]

Henry Cook died September 17, 1824, at the age of 55, one month short of the 30th anniversary of his installation. In recording the event the

Session called him a "much beloved pastor," and the congregation, in grateful respect, erected a stone tablet over his grave in the old burial ground.[27] He was an effective leader, who earned and maintained the love and respect of his congregation, and who always put the interests of the people above his own personal concerns. In 1794 the future of the little congregation was uncertain, and the disputes occurring at the time of separation from the First Church of Woodbridge had caused widespread bitterness and controversy. Many factors helped to assure the firm establishment of the new congregation, and some of these were beyond the influence of one church. The growth of a national, interdenominational evangelical mission activity helped to create the soil to nourish the new church. The community of Metuchen itself became more populous and more active after 1810 when the new turnpikes between Newark and New Brunswick, and between Bound Brook and Perth Amboy crossed at Metuchen and made the community a center of travel routes that has marked its entire subsequent history.[28] But under less effective leadership, and with a less determined congregation, the church might have missed the opportunity, not only to heal the wounds caused by the separation of the congregations, but to grow and prosper in its own right. It was under Henry Cook that it became certain that the history of the church and the history of the community of which it was a part would be linked together for many decades to come.

STATISTICS

Cook

> *Marriages* — 361 (about 13 were marriages of negros, most of whom were slaves)
>
> *Baptisms* (beginning December, 1816) — 57
>
> *Total admissions* — 257

CHAPTER XI — FOOTNOTES

1. Session minutes, October 3, 1825.
2. Ezra M. Hunt, *History of the Churches of Metuchen, N. J.,* 1870, 9-10; Rev. J. G. Mason, *History of Metuchen,* New Brunswick, N. J., 62, 64; Helen Wright, *The First Presbyterian Congregation, Mendham, Morris County, New Jersey,* Jersey City 1939, 221.
3. *Metuchen, The Brainy Borough,* unpublished, ch. 2, p. 1-2 (hereafter referred to as Library Manuscript).
4. Clifton E. Olmstead, *Religion in America, Past and Present,* Englewood Cliffs, New Jersey 1961, 54-5; W. W. Sweet, *The Story of Religion in America,* New York, 1930, 324; Leonard J. Trinterud, *The Forming of An American Tradition,* Philadelphia, 1949, 261-8.
5. Irving S. Kull, ed., *New Jersey, A History,* New York 1930, II, 517.
6. The two Freemans and Bloomfield were elders of the Woodbridge Church; James Manning, Bloomfield and Matthew Freeman were also deacons. See extract from minutes of the Woodbridge Session, May 13, 1788 and March 12, 1791.
7. Session minutes, June 27, 1795; May 9, 1797; April 14 and October 25, 1798; September 28, 1799. The death of James Manning in 1797 meant that the church's membership in 1800 was 80.
8. Trustees minutes, January 1 and 6, 1795; April 17, 1795; March 30, 1796. The location was on the east side of Main Street, opposite Durham Avenue.
9. Trustees minutes, April 30, 1796.
10. The progress of this dispute may be followed in Trustees minutes during the year 1795, May 6, 1797, and September 8, 1800. See also minutes of congregation meeting May 28, 1801. The church possesses a copy of the decision of the Court of Appeals.
11. Trustees minutes, March 7, 1803; February 12, 1812.
12. A distinctive seal of the 2nd Presbyterian Church had already been adopted in 1799. See Trustees minutes, May 6 and July 15, 1799.
13. Olmstead, *op. cit.,* 62-3; 66-7; Sweet, *op. cit.,* 329 ff.

14. Sweet, *op. cit.,* 326-7, 357, 366-7. The cooperation between Presbyterians and Congregationalists had been expressed in the Plan of Union in 1801.
15. Session minutes, October 15, 1803; May 5, 1804; September 27, 1806. A few of the members were negro slaves. Dinah, a Black Woman, was admitted in 1803; Nance, a Black Woman, in 1804. Will, a Black Man, was disciplined by Session in 1807.
16. Session minutes, July 25, 1814; September 9 and 16, 1815.
17. Session minutes, October 15, 1814.
18. Session minutes, April 29, 1806.
19. Session minutes, April21, 1810.
20. Session minutes, May 6, 1815.
21. William H. Ayers, *A History of the First Presbyterian Church, Metuchen,* 1947, p. 20. Library Manuscript, *op. cit.,* ch. 10, p. 4; ch. 11, p. 4. The early Sunday School may have offered a combination of religious and secular instruction. See Olmstead, *op. cit.,* p. 73.
22. Session minutes, April 8, 1818, and Membership Roll. 73 of the 118 were women. The membership roll lists 88 on April 11 (Saturday), 2 on April 12. Session minutes record 80 persons received on April 8, 7 on April 11, 3 on April 12, for a total of 90. The other 28 were admitted in June and October. The figure of 90 was not surpassed until 1960 and later, when total admissions during Holy Week exceeded 90.
23. Mason, *op. cit.,* quoting Joel Campbell, p. 64; Hunt, *op. cit.,* 17.
24. Pew rents are listed in the minutes of the meetings of the Board of Trustees. Figures cited are from minutes of various meetings.
25. Minutes of congregation meeting April 17, 1805; Trustees minutes, April 9 and May 19, 1807.
26. Minutes of congregation meeting, April 28, 1808; May 2, 1814. John Martin was the first chorister.
27. Session minutes, November 6, 1824. At the same meeting the Session received his daughter Rebecca into the church.
28. Library Manuscript, ch. 2, p. 3; ch. on Business, p. 3-5. Hunt, *Metuchen and Her History,* New York 1870, 16.

Chapter XII

OSBORN, HUNT, BURGHARDT 1825-1850

"The new meeting house the foundation stone of which was laid early in the fall of 1835 was solemnly dedicated to the worship of Almighty God January 30, 1836."
  – Note in Session minutes, vol. II, p. 87

The railroad is expected to pass just below the Meeting House hill, entering church land at the northwest corner of the burial ground.... The new church, to be completed by November, is to be patterned after the Presbyterian Church of New Providence.
  – Paraphrase of letter of Richard Ross to his children,
  April 13, 1835

THE QUARTER CENTURY after 1825 was to bring important changes, both in the church and in the community which it served. It was during this period that both the present church building and the present manse were built. The new church was desirable to accommodate a larger congregation, and made immediately urgent by the coming of the New Jersey Railroad on its way from Jersey City to New Brunswick, and the prospect of the track entering church property. It was in this period too that Presbyterians everywhere as well as other Christians faced for the first time the moral issue of negro slavery, an issue which aroused bitter controversy, destroyed interdenominational cooperation, and split the church into two competing national jurisdictions. The Old School General Assembly, which came ultimately to defend the institution of negro slavery, included the churches of the Presbytery of Elizabethtown.

A congregation meeting on December 12, 1824, elected Rev. Michael Osborn pastor, at a salary of $400, payable quarterly, with use of the parsonage house and lot. He was ordained and installed on February 23, 1825, remaining a little more than two years, until June 26, 1827, when at his own request the Presbytery of Elizabethtown dissolved the pastoral relation.[1] Osborn, a native of New Jersey, was in the Class of 1822 at Princeton Theological Seminary. The Metuchen ministry may have been the first for the 29 year old pastor; after he left in 1827 his ministerial career spanned another 35 years in a variety of churches, mostly in the South. Like his predecessor, he had a reputation as a classical scholar. His preaching was characterized as of the highest order of excellence, emphasizing an intellectual appeal rather than emotional oratory. Introspective in personality, he was described as having a high standard of moral integrity and a strong sense of duty and responsibility.[2]

Osborn's brief pastorate was a constructive one. His main effort appeared to be to bring new responsibilities to the Session, both in sharing the work of pastoral visiting, and in providing for more systematic observance of the sacrament of communion. Four new elders were elected in 1825, Samuel Bloodgood, Melanthon Mundy, Enos Talmage, and Amos Noe, raising the membership of Session to eight elders.[3] In the fall of 1826 the Session divided the congregation into seven districts, and assigned individual elders to each district, to accompany the pastor on his weekly visits.[4]

Other efforts were made to make the members more aware of their Christian duties. The Session decided to hold communion four times a year, on the first Sundays of March, June, September and December.[5] It also began the practice of occasionally setting aside a special day of prayer. One was designated for Saturday, June 3, 1826, ... "as a day of special humiliation and fasting before God, with prayer for the pardon of our many sins, and for a gracious effusion of the Divine Spirit upon the Church and congregation ..."[6] A worship service was scheduled for 4 o'clock that day. As this event indicates, Saturday was sometimes used for religious purposes, a role it has since clearly lost among Protestants. The Session frequently met on that day, especially when new members were to be admitted.

The gradually increasing responsibilities of the Session were making it more truly the layman's governing body of the church. This process had begun in the latter part of Cook's ministry, perhaps with the decision to found and hence to supervise a Sunday School, and it received considerable impetus during this brief pastorate of Michael Osborn.

The minister whose career spanned most of this period was Holloway Whitfield Hunt, whose service at Metuchen came after a brief period in another church outside the state. A descendant of Augustine Hunt who had given his name to Hunt's Point on the north shore of Long Island, Holloway Hunt was born in Hunderdon County, New Jersey, the son of a minister. He graduated from the College of New Jersey in 1818, and from Princeton Theological Seminary in 1822, in the same class as Michael Osborn. He studied for a time under Dr. Robert Finley of Basking Ridge, whose son was to come to the Metuchen pulpit in 1850. Licensed by the Presbytery of Newton, Hunt preached for a short time at a church in Albany, New York, before coming to Metuchen. Hunt supplied the pulpit temporarily in the fall and winter of 1827, then was called as the pastor and formally installed on April 29, 1828, just 111 years after the installation of John Pierson in the Woodbridge pulpit.[7]

His nineteen years as pastor, though his final years were marked by controversy and he left amid divided feelings in the congregation, were sufficiently long for him to consider Metuchen his home. In 1829 he married Henrietta Mundy; one of his sons, Dr. Ezra Hunt, not only became a prominent physician, but also wrote a history of Metuchen and a history of its churches, both of which have come to be an important part of the record of the past.[8] His other son Theodore became a professor of English at Princeton, and was instrumental in the founding of the Metuchen Public Library. After leaving Metuchen in 1847 he ministered for ten years to the Congregational Church at Patchogue, Long Island, and then went to the Presbyterian Church in Centreville, Orange County, New York. He later returned to Metuchen and built a home on Middlesex Avenue, which subsequently became the Ramble Inn. There he spent the last years of his life until his death in 1882. The graves of the minister, his wife, and his son Ezra, are in the southwest area of the church's burial ground.

Probably the most important event of Hunt's pastorate was the coming of the railroad which was to have important influence on both church and community. As the railroad company bought up land for its right of way, it became apparent that the line of track would run through the area where the parishioners tied their horses while they attended service, and would come so close to the existing church that the new one would have to be built in another location.[9]

The movement to build a new church had begun in 1834 under the leadership of Stelle Manning and William M. Ross, merchants who had recently moved to Metuchen from New York. The land on which the present church, cemetery and manse are located was bought that same year from John Hampton, Sr., at $30 an acre. Well before the coming of the railroad the decision to build a new and larger church had been made by the congregation. Specific plans had been made by the spring of 1835. The new church was to be 60' x 40', based upon the plan of the church at New Providence. The old building was to be taken down in May, and the new one completed in November at an expected cost of about $3,500.[10] Then, rather suddenly, the imminence of railroad construction gave the whole matter a new urgency. Whether the location of the railroad would necessitate a new site for the church became a question of immediate concern. A congregation meeting was called for May 25, 1835 in order to debate the question, and a committee was appointed to determine damages to be sustained to church property in the course of building the railroad.[11] Though the need for a new church had been realized earlier, the location of the railroad helped to determine the site where the church would be built.

Once the decision on location had been made the work proceeded rapidly. The new church, larger than the old, with a small cupola, was dedicated January 30, 1836.[12] Though it has undergone a number of modifications since that time, it is still the same building that serves the present congregation. Almost $4,000 was raised by special subscription, and the old building sold to Lewis Thomas for $175. Solomon Brothers, the contractors, were paid $3,530, and Jonathan Thompson $60 for stones.[13] Some unforeseen later expense must have occurred when the church was entered and the carpeting taken up and removed. The Board of Trustees advertised a $75 reward for recovery of the property and conviction of the thief.[14] The New Jersey Railroad was completed through Metuchen late in 1836, Campbell's station built near the crossing of the turnpikes, and a few years later another station constructed at Main Street. The day the first train came in the village school adjourned to the church grounds, the onlookers growing impatient and excited during the hour they had to wait. Ezra Hunt recalls that "... one stout young miss ... screamed and ran quite a distance ..." because she was so frightened by the locomotive.[15]

The building of a railroad station at Main Street was a recognition that the center of Metuchen was not to be at the crossroads of the turnpikes. John Hampton and Lewis Campbell had earlier built rival inns at the crossroads, but that area grew very little compared with the growth that occurred on Main Street itself. Along that street between the Amboy Turnpike and Durham Avenue there were some 14 buildings by the end of the forties, and some further growth along the Middlesex Turnpike near Main.[16] The location of the church was central to this orientation, and as the community grew so did the activities of the church as its primary social and religious center. Farmers from the area beyond the business district composed the great majority of the congregation. A Wood Bee or Minister's Frolic was held in October, a traditional social occasion for the serving of chicken pie and coffee, but also with the serious purpose of filling up the minister's wood pile before the coming of winter. Salt Water Day came in August, with a picnic at Florida Grove. After the Raritan Hotel was built in the 1850s, the party would go there for dancing.[17] Alpheus W. Kellogg came in 1839, and for the next 30 years was in charge of music at the church, and taught at Franklin School. For a time he organized a separate music school at New Durham, and did much to foster the musical tastes of the people.[18]

The activities of Session continued to revolve mainly around the admission of new members and the disciplining of old ones. One parishioner, charged with intemperance and "absenting himself from the social and public means of grace" was suspended from communion until he gave evidence of repentance and reformation.[19] Lewis Thomas, prominent merchant and postmaster, was charged with using abusive and profane language against a fellow member, and was required to make public confession of his sorrow and ask forgiveness.[20] Another was cited for drunkenness on the day of the township election and was suspended from the communion of the church.[21] These matters occurred frequently enough so that there could be no doubt whatever of what the church considered to be the proper standards of behavior, nor could any parishioner doubt that the church had the power to uphold its standards.

The Presbytery of Elizabethtown, to which the church has belonged ever since its organization in 1824, took steps to supervise the activities of its member churches. It required them to keep their session minutes in a substantial and durable book, and in 1828 began the practice of examining and approving session minutes at regular intervals.[22] After the building of the new church the Session was increased to ten members, with the election of four new elders: Stelle Manning, Daniel Voorhees, John Henry Campbell, and William Ross.[23]

Accessions to membership during Hunt's pastorate came in bunches. During the late summer and fall of 1831, 35 new members, almost all women, joined the church; 25 in 1832, of whom 21 were women. On the other hand, only 16 had joined in the six years prior to 1831; only two came in 1835, one in 1836.

The banner year for new members was 1843. On May 14, 47 new communicants were accepted and 10 more came in August, the total of 57 being surpassed only by the revival year of 1818. Among these new family names began to be encountered: Long, Black, Sofield, Vansickle, King, Laforge.[24] Unlike the earlier time, however, these new additions did not do much more than replace those who had died or left the church. By the end of Hunt's tenure, the membership was barely over 200, practically unchanged from 25 years before.[25]

Collections from pew rents did not change radically through these years, though there was always some annual fluctuation. Amounts to be collected were apportioned out among five or six trustees, each acting as collector from a certain number of the members. The lists of amounts due the collectors who in turn gave the money to the Board of Trustees are preserved in a book covering the years 1824 to 1859. For these purposes the church year began on May 1. Pew rent totals in 1824-6 were, respectively, $374, 360 and 396.[26] In 1833 and 1834 the amounts were $374 and $372; in 1844-6, $334, 345 and 307. The lesser amounts in the forties may have resulted from the controversy of those years over Hunt's continued pastorate. Since the minister's salary through these years remained at $400, pew rents had to be supplemented by collections at church services and occasional special subscriptions.

Presbyterians and Protestants of other denominations were deeply concerned in these years over the moral issue of slavery. The old certainty that had once characterized the church's position began to be challenged by the 1820s. There was serious disagreement too over the desirability of continuing the interdenominational cooperation that had earlier proved an effective vehicle for the mission of Protestantism in an expanding America. As time went on the quarrels became more serious, the earlier tolerance became more rigid dogmatism leading to schism within churches and to the appearance of new religious sects, and reflecting the sectional differences that were rising in the nation which were eventually to prove beyond the power of democracy to heal peacefully.

The moral responsibility of the individual so strongly emphasized by Puritanism made it natural for the policy making bodies of the church to take a stand against the continued existence of negro slavery. In 1818 the General Assembly unanimously adopted a resolution calling slavery inconsistent with the Law of God and the Gospel of Christ; it was the duty of all Christians to work for the complete abolition of slavery.[27] Further efforts to provide for continued action by the General Assembly were unsuccessful, however. The increasing importance of the southern cotton economy based on slavery, coupled with the increasingly violent attacks upon slavery by northern abolitionist crusaders, led by William Lloyd Garrison, and centered in the numerous anti-slavery societies, meant that national church bodies were unable to secure consensus on any policy. Anti-slavery pronouncements were buried in committee, and there began to be some justification of slavery from the pulpit.[28]

Meanwhile the increasing sectionalism of the 1830s brought to a head a growing theological dispute over the value of interdenominational cooperation. The earlier Plan of Union of 1801 which had united the frontier mission work of Congregationalists and Presbyterians came under increasingly critical scrutiny. The Scotch-Irish Presbyterians in particular, whose numbers had grown through immigration, wanted a stricter denominational control of mission work. Other factors, mainly theological in nature, exacerbated the dispute. Finally in 1837, the General Assembly, controlled by its more orthodox elements, dissolved the Plan of Union and expelled four full synods, which had been organized under the plan, from the church.[29] Those synods formed their own General Assembly, constituting the New School Presbyterian Church, while the original General Assembly, shorn of a significant fraction of its membership, constituted the Old School Presbyterian Church.

It was in the Old School Church, with the strength of its membership in the older settled areas of the east and south, that the greatest tolerance to negro slavery was shown. The major reason was the desire of conservatives to avoid an outbreak of violence and possible revolution over the slavery question; abolition, it was felt, would promote dissension and would be more likely to hurt rather than help the negro's cause. Charles Hodge of Princeton Theological Seminary was the most important Presbyterian spokesman for this conservative point of view. To him the Bible did not condemn slavery nor did Christ or the Apostles call for its abolition, though he hoped that eventually, slavery would die out.[30] Other conservatives found authority for defending slavery on scriptural and moral grounds, or at least thought that the General Assembly ought to take no stand at all on the question. Though the New School General Assembly actively opposed slavery, both organizations were eventually to split north and south because of the Civil War. It should be noted, however, that when the sectional controversy erupted into secession and war, the Old School churches of the north patriotically supported the Lincoln administration. In 1861 its General Assembly passed such a resolution, introduced by a strong conservative on the slavery issue, Dr. Gardner Spring, pastor of the Brick Presbyterian Church of New York.[31]

How these matters affected the congregation of the Second Presbyterian Church of Woodbridge is not recorded, but it is worth noting that as an Old School church, the leadership and higher authority to which it looked for inspiration and guidance took its stand against the earlier statements of the General Assembly, unable any longer to say what had once

109

been so clear as Christian doctrine, that slavery was inconsistent with the Law of God and the Gospel of Christ. There could be no better illustration that the church was a creature of its times, unable to free itself sufficiently from the interests of its people to provide a clear and united stand on one of the most fundamental issues that the nation has ever faced.

The last years of the pastorate of Holloway Whitfield Hunt were marked by controversy. On April 23, 1844, Hunt requested permission from the Presbytery to resign his charge and on May 7, the Presbytery formally dissolved the pastoral connection.[32] However, at a Session meeting on June 17, four elders, Simeon Mundy, Richard Ross, Melanthon Mundy and John Henry Campbell, charging that Hunt had originated false reports about them which were circulating in the congregation, offered their resignations as active members of Session.[33] Session accepted the resignations, recognizing that the four had become "unacceptable to a part of the people." The reason for the division within the congregation is not clear, though it may have arisen from the fact that Hunt was the executor of the estate of his father-in-law, Ezra Mundy.[34] A congregation meeting scheduled in September, for the purpose of selecting a new pastor, was postponed until October, and again put off until the next spring.[35] Finally the congregation on April 15, 1845, voted to call Rev. John McDowell; but in June he refused the call.[36]

A second congregation meeting, held September 30, 1845, voted to invite Rev. Hunt to return to the pulpit, but a minority who were opposed appointed their own commissioners to Presbytery. Accordingly, when Presbytery met on October 8, it was confronted by differing requests from opposed commissioners, with the logical result that Presbytery refused to put the call in Hunt's hands.[37] The congregation, through its majority, then appealed to the Synod of New Jersey to reverse the decision of the Presbytery of Elizabethtown. The Synod, on October 23, 1845, upheld the complaint of the congregation, stating that it expressed no opinion on the merits of the dispute, but simply felt that there was not

110

sufficient ground to refuse the majority permission to call Rev. Hunt. The Presbytery, accepting Synod's reversal of its earlier action, then scheduled a meeting at Metuchen for November 25 for the purpose of learning whether or not the pastor would accept the call.

Just before the meeting was held two more elders, William Ross and Daniel Voorhees resigned, reducing the active Session to two elders, Samuel Bloodgood and Stelle Manning. Their letter of resignation said that the earlier action of four elders had not accomplished its purpose, and that Hunt and his friends continued to urge further resignations. These resignations were accepted as an effort to restore peace and harmony in the congregation, and were not to be construed as reflecting on the Christian behavior of those who resigned.[38] When Presbytery met at Metuchen as scheduled, it was presented with a petition against the installation of Rev. Hunt, signed by 42 members, almost all heads of families. Before Presbytery could take further action, the parties to the disagreement after consultation agreed to the compromise that they would consent to Hunt's appointment as stated supply for 17 months, until May 1, 1847, on condition that Hunt cease his ministry on or before that date. Under these conditions, Hunt returned.

Irrespective of the cause of the controversy, it is apparent that most of the elders and a large majority of the congregation were opposed to Hunt's continuing in the pulpit. That he was willing to come to such a divided congregation hardly speaks well for his sense of judgment. His usefulness as a pastor had ended in 1844. After he returned, there was only one Session meeting during the rest of his tenure, and the two elders who constituted the Session could obviously do nothing to carry on the work of the church. The large increase in membership that had come in 1843 did not become a permanent enlargement, and the collections from pew rents declined. It was unfortunate that the long and important ministry of Holloway Whitfield Hunt should have ended in bitterness and controversy.

The congregation called Rev. Peter H. Burghardt to the pulpit in October, 1847, and he was installed on November 30, remaining at Metuchen until June 5, 1850. Burghardt was a native of Massachusetts who had come to the ministry relatively late in life. He graduated from Auburn (New York) Theological Seminary in 1843 and had his first ministry in Michigan before coming to Metuchen at the age of 38. After leaving Metuchen he preached for a time in New York State; then when the Civil War came his desire to do Christian service where it was greatly needed led him to become a chaplain with the Army of the Potomac. His son Charles was killed in the war.[39]

Burghardt did what he could to heal the wounds of the previous years. The Session was put once again on a firm basis with the election of three new elders, John H. Campbell (who had resigned in 1844), Benajah Mundy, and David Bloomfield; Burghardt not only presided over the meetings of Session but was the first minister to sign the minutes.[40] In February, 1848, the Session decided that in accepting members transferring from other churches, their assent to "the articles and covenant of this church" be required. The first two members admitted under this policy were Mr. Albert Edgar from the Spring Street Presbyterian Church of New York, and Mrs. Eliza Jackson Burghardt, the pastor's wife, from the First Presbyterian Church of Plymouth, Michigan.[41]

The present manse was built during Burghardt's time. The report of the building committee in 1849 showed the cost of the house, barn and fences as $2,325.22. A subscription taken in the congregation did not cover the entire cost, however, and a note and mortgage had to be issued for the unpaid balance of $950.36.[42] Like the church itself, the manse, though modified in certain respects in later years, has served as the home of each of the ministers since, and has in more recent years become one of the notable buildings in the community.

Chapter XII

STATISTICS

Osborn
    Marriages — 24 (1 of a free negro to a slave woman)
    Baptisms — 11
    Total Admissions — 7

Hunt
    Marriages — 64 (5 colored)
    Baptisms — 76
    Total Admissions — 198

Burghardt
    Marriages — 17
    Baptisms — 14
    Total Admissions — 28

CHAPTER XII – FOOTNOTES

1. Ezra M. Hunt, *History of the Churches of Metuchen*, New York 1870, p. 13-14.
2. James C. Mason, *A History of Metuchen*, New Brunswick, N. J., p. 65, quoting another clergyman's opinion.
3. Session minutes, November 26, 1825. For most of Cook's ministry the Session comprised six or seven elders, but there was no systematic replacement of those who died or left the church. After these additions in 1825, no elders were added to the Session until 1839.
4. Session minutes November 13, 1826.
5. Session minutes May 26, August 1, 1825.
6. Session minutes, May 26, 1826.
7. Biographical information is in Hunt, *op. cit.*, 14; *Encyclopedia of the Presbyterian Church in the U.S.A.*, 1884, p. 357. See also notes on p. 34 and 36 of Session minutes, vol. II.
8. Ezra Hunt was one of the leaders in the movement to create a State Board of Health in the 1870s.
9. Statement of a committee of the congregation (no date); note of William H. Ayers referring to a communication from the committee to the railroad company in 1835. See also William H. Ayers, *A History of the First Presbyterian Church of Metuchen*, Metuchen, N. J., 1947, 21-2.
10. Letter of Richard Ross to his children, April 13, 1835.
11. Ayers, *op. cit.*, 21-2. The subject is mentioned also in Library manuscript, *op. cit.*, ch. 11, p. 5.
12. Note in Session minutes, II, 87.
13. Transcribed note made by William H. Ayers in 1947 of the record of Simeon Mundy, Treasurer of the Building Committee; Mason, *op. cit.*, 65-6. The beams from the old structure became part of a house subsequently located at 484 Middlesex Avenue. See Ayers, *op. cit.*, 22.
14. Advertisement, dated June 13, 1838, inserted in *The Fredonian*, New Brunswick, July 4, 1838; information taken from notes of J. Lloyd Grimstead.
15. Ezra Hunt, *Metuchen and Her History*, New York 1870, 21.

16. Library manuscript, *op. cit.*, ch. 2, pgs. 4-6; ch. on business, pgs. 4-5. The business development was on the west side of Main Street. The crossroads of the turnpikes was probably at the present intersection of Middlesex Avenue, New Durham Road and Memorial Parkway.

17. Library manuscript, *op. cit.*, ch. on business, p. 7; Hunt, *op. cit.*, 22.

18. Hunt, *op. cit.*, 22; Library Manuscript, *op. cit.*, ch. 10, p. 5; notes of William H. Ayers.

19. Session minutes February 14, March 16, 1832.

20. Session minutes November 28, 1839.

21. Session minutes November 13, 1840.

22. See front fly leaf of Session Book, Vol. II for copy of resolution of Presbytery; the first minutes were approved for Presbytery in September, 1828. See also Herbert K. England, *Historical Sketch of the Presbytery of Elizabeth,* June 1925. Elizabethtown was shortened to Elizabeth in 1870.

23. Session minutes, July 14, 1839.

24. Membership roll in Session Book, vol. I; Session minutes, May 13, August 12, 1843.

25. 206 was reported to Presbytery as of April 1849; see membership roll, Session Book, vol. II.

26. Book containing copies of the lists of pew rent to be collected by the Trustees of the 2nd Church of Woodbridge. Amounts are rounded to the nearest dollar.

27. Gaius J. Slosser, ed., *They Seek a Country: The American Presbyterians,* 1955, 220-1; William W. Sweet, *The Story of Religion in America,* Harper 1930, 423.

28. Sweet, *op cit.,* 424-6.

29. Sweet, *op. cit.,* 377-9; Clifton Olmstead, *Religion in America, Past and Present,* Englewood Cliffs, N. J., 1961, 79-80; Wallace N. Jamison, *Religion in New Jersey: A Brief History,* Princeton 1964, 95-6. Other churches were also undergoing similar experiences in these years. See Sweet, *op. cit.,* 440-4.

30. Olmstead, *op. cit.,* 95; Jamison, *op. cit.,* 102. Hodge's influence made Princeton Seminary the seat of conservatism. When Union Seminary was founded in New York in 1836 it rapidly became the center of more liberal views.

115

31. Sweet, *op. cit.,* 449.

32. Session Book, II, 132.

33. Session minutes, June 17, 1844. Campbell came back to the Session after Hunt left to serve 14 years.

34. Transcript by W. H. Ayers of Mundy's History, ch. 3.

35. Session minutes, September 13, 17, 1844.

36. Session minutes, April 15, June 11, 1845. McDowell had been pastor of the First Presbyterian Church of Elizabeth, 1804-1832, then went to Central Presbyterian Church in Philadelphia. See Theodore Thayer, *As We Were: The Story of Old Elizabethtown,* Elizabeth, N. J. 1964, 213-214.

37. Session minutes, September 30, 1845; and Session Book, II, 152-157 for actions of Presbytery and Synod.

38. Session minutes, November 13, 1845. Ross returned to the Session under Rev. Plumley to serve another 10 years.

39. Hunt, *History of the Churches of Metuchen, op. cit.,* 15.

40. Session minutes, December 26, 1847.

41. Session minutes, February 12, 1848.

42. Ayers, *op. cit.,* 23; Hunt, *Metuchen and Her History, op. cit.,* 23.

Chapter XIII

FINLEY, PLUMLEY 1850-1875

The petitioners for a congregation meeting were charged "by public rumor with unChristian conduct in disturbing the peace of the Church by the manner and spirit in which they engaged in a Festival held on the Fourth of July last, for the purpose of raising funds for the Church ..."
— Session minutes, December 29, 1856

"Whereas by recommendation of the President of the United States, the last Thursday in September has been designated as a day of national fasting and prayer and as the present state of our country is such as to call for fervent prayer, therefore Resolved that the Session earnestly request the members of this congregation to observe the day in accordance with the recommendation; and, for that purpose, to assemble, as on the Lord's Day, at the church at 10 1/2 o'clock, in the morning, and at the Lecture Room, at 7 o'clock in the evening."
— Session minutes, September 13, 1861

"The Session does not approve the use of [the Church and the Lecture Room] for business associations, elections, primary meetings of political parties, or the exhibition of singers or showmen for which purposes the public hail can be obtained, and no one of which need be accommodated upon the church premises."
— Session minutes, February 24, 1873

THE THIRD QUARTER of the 19th century was a time of trial for the Metuchen Church. For the first time a dispute within the congregation became so serious that a large number of people withdrew in order to form a new fellowship, the Reformed Church. For the first time, too, the Presbyterian Church ceased to be the only church in the community, when in the years immediately after the Civil War three new churches were founded, St. Luke's Episcopal, Centenary Methodist, and St. Francis Roman Catholic. The controversial ministry of Rev. Robert Finley in the 1850s ultimately brought a significant decline in church membership, so that from the late years of the '50s until after the Civil War the membership was less than 175, reaching its lowest point in 1860, with 131 communicants, the smallest membership in 55 years.

In the post-Civil War years, the second half of the pastorate of Rev. Gardiner Spring Plumley, the vitality and strength of the church reasserted itself. Membership increased significantly to well above 250 in the early 1870s, and the activities of the church expanded with the growth of the community. Finally, in the first year of Rev. Plumley's ministry, the church adopted its present name, the First Presbyterian Church of Metuchen.

In the fall of 1850 the congregation called Rev. Robert Smith Finley to the pulpit; he was installed November 14, 1850, remaining just short of seven years until October, 1857. His father, the Presbyterian minister at Basking Ridge, was widely known as the author of a colonization plan for the settlement of freed slaves in Africa, and also served as headmaster of the Academy at Basking Ridge. Like his father, the son was clearly interested in education as well as religion. But like Burghardt, Finley came to the ministry indirectly. He graduated from the College of New Jersey in 1821, then studied law and practiced in Cincinnati, Ohio, before deciding to enter the ministry.[1]

Finley's greatest contributions to the growth of the church came in his early years. He was apparently a man of great zeal, with outspoken

118

and forceful ideas, and for a time he succeeded in attracting more people to his sermons. The fact that the main body of the church as well as the gallery could on occasion be almost filled eventually led to a decision to enlarge the seating capacity of the church, and this addition was made in 1857.[2]

Finley's interest in education was centered in his desire to establish a parochial school under church sponsorship. This academy movement, as it was sometimes called, was particularly strong in the Old School Presbyterian Church during the 1840s. The Old School General Assembly had urged the establishment of parochial schools, and the Synod of New Jersey had recommended that such schools be supported by public taxation.[3] Thirty-six parochial schools were founded by the Old School Church. In Metuchen the enterprising Finley established the Parochial Academy in 1852, located on the Amboy turnpike until 1858 when it was moved to the church grounds.[4] The minister taught boys at the Academy, while his wife Julia conducted a female seminary at the parsonage.[5] A prospectus of the school in 1856 listed Philip S. Caffrey, a Princeton graduate, as principal and proprietor. The two terms began in May and November and tuition was $125 each term. The school's purpose was to prepare boys for college or business.[6] When the Presbyterian Church as a whole turned its attention to the support of public schools after the Civil War, many of the parochial schools ceased to exist and the academy movement died out. In Metuchen private education continued to be widely used through the 19th century. A series of small private schools occupied the Academy building, and Mr. Marshall's school for boys and girls flourished between 1868 and 1886.[7]

One other change instituted by Finley may be more briefly mentioned. In the spring of 1853 when three new elders were elected, a Board of Deacons was also created. The first three deacons were David Thomas, John J. Clarkson and John Watson.[8] An effort to elect three more in 1857 was defeated by the controversy raging at the time. Rev. Plumley, who succeeded Finley, evidently allowed the Board to cease its activity, since there is no further word of it for another 25 years; nor do we know what the duties of the deacons were supposed to be. At any rate it is clear that Finley made positive contributions to his church and community before the quarrel arose that destroyed the peace and unity of the congregation.

The origins of the bad feeling that disrupted the congregation are not fully recorded, partly because of the destruction of a section of the Session minutes, on Presbytery's recommendation. It may have begun in the need to raise money for refurnishing the church after the expansion of the building had been planned for. A festival was held on July 4, 1856, for the purpose of raising such funds, and when the behavior of some prominent members at the festival became the subject of public rumor and criticism, the pastor declared that he would not walk on a carpet that had been purchased with festival money.[9]

Whatever happened at the picnic, the Session delayed taking any action to investigate the rumors and to discipline any individuals. Finally in November 1856 a petition signed by 27 members was presented to Session asking for a congregational meeting. The Session refused the request, and then learned that some of the petitioners had been accused, presumably by the pastor, of "unChristian conduct in disturbing the peace of the church by the manner and spirit in which they engaged in a Festival held on the Fourth of July last ..."[10] The individuals involved were Lewis Thomas, Dr. Ezra Hunt, John Clarkson, Dayton Decker, and Melanthon Mundy. Thomas was a trustee, and Clarkson a deacon; Mundy was on the Session at the time of the dispute with Holloway Whitfield Hunt. A Session committee, appointed to talk with the individuals and to take whatever remedial action might be called for, found the accused unwilling to say that they had done anything wrong.[11] Efforts to bring them before Session to answer the charges proved equally unsuccessful.[12]

The dispute was further aggravated when the Session decided on July 31, 1857, to recommend to the congregation the election of four more elders and three more deacons. One of the elders, John Henry Campbell, tried unsuccessfully to get Session to postpone the election. It was scheduled for August 8, but then was prevented from being held "by the disorderly conduct of certain persons in the assembly."[13] The Trustees, on the advice of the dissident group, ordered the church to be closed on the third, fourth and fifth Sundays of August to prevent any congregation meeting.

By this time the issue had made strong partisans on both sides, and it was clearly jeopardizing the unity of the congregation. Letters appeared in the press, anonymously or with pseudonyms, attacking or defending the pastor. In defense of Rev. Finley, an anonymous writer said that the "dislikes and slanders against the pastor ... are entirely groundless." His effective preaching and his devotion to charity and the needs of the poor were cited. In his services for the moral and intellectual education of youth, "he is proving himself a blessing to his age ..."; there was praise not only for the academy for boys and his wife's seminary for girls, but also for the active Sunday School and Bible Class. Rev. Finley held no prejudice toward his opponents, even as he was, "by their hostilities, driven from the use of his pulpit, and the doors of his church closed against him." The only solution, thought this writer, was to await the action of Presbytery.[14]

On the other side, one of his attackers called Rev. Finley a man of "pugnacious disposition" who had committed "frauds and abuses," "a plotter of mischief," and "the only cause of disturbance in our peaceful village." Signing himself "Veritas," the writer quoted with obvious approval the action of Presbytery in dissolving the pastoral connection and the refusal of Synod to sustain his appeal.[15]

In this highly charged atmosphere there could be no compromise solution. In connection with the recent election and the closing of the church, the Session charged improper conduct against Messrs. Mundy, Thomas, Decker and Hunt, who had been previously cited for disturbing the peace of the church, and in addition, John Henry Campbell, himself an elder, and William Ross.[16] All were cited to appear before Session, and all refused. The only action that Session could take was to suspend Campbell's privilege of voting and hear his case separately.[17] Further details on the nature of the dispute cannot be ascertained, because Session, on Presbytery's declaration that the proceedings were inconclusive and certain unrecorded testimony was null and void, ordered certain pages of the minutes destroyed. This action might be an indication that the dispute at bottom rested more on personality clashes than on matters of policy or organization, or legal authority to close the church.

The whole matter came to a head in October, 1857. The Presbytery of Elizabethtown directed Session to suspend the trial of members under discipline and to show cause why the pastoral relationship should not be dissolved.[18] Rev. Finley appealed to Synod, and on Synod's refusal to support the pastor, Presbytery informed Session that it "must regard any interference thereafter of Mr. Finley in the concerns of the Second Church of Woodbridge, as subjecting him to the censure of Presbytery."[19] The significance of this action lies in the fact that the Presbytery found more fault in Finley than in any action by the members under discipline. Two of the accused, Ezra Hunt and William Ross, shortly were seated as new elders at a Session meeting, November 7, 1857, presided over by two ministers from Presbytery, and Campbell was restored to his Sessional privileges. This hardly indicates that the charges against these men had much substance. Campbell, a trustee, served four more years as an elder, Ross ten years, and Hunt sixteen. Mundy, Thomas and Ross served successively as Presidents of the Board of Trustees. It is the apparent lack of any other important issue than personality that makes this dispute so different from the dispute over parsonage rights in the 1790s. In that case there was at least something to argue about. Yet these matters aroused

122

sufficient passion to cause certain members to withdraw from the church in order to participate in the organization of the new Reformed Church.

A long session meeting on November 7, 1857, began the process of recovery and reorganization. Three new elders were seated, William Ross, Ezra Hunt and John Watson; two others, Albert Edgar and Smith Bloomfield, requested and received certificates of dismissal in order to join the Reformed Church. Session then drew up a statement citing previous misunderstandings and honest differences of opinion and resolved to dismiss the cases arising from the famous Fourth of July picnic and from the subsequent effort to elect new elders and deacons and the closing of the church. The resolution ended with an appeal for mutual confidence and forgiveness. It was adopted unanimously by the three remaining elders who had not been directly involved.[20]

Shortly thereafter, on November 10, 1857, 51 members of the church drew up an agreement which stated:

> "The undersigned, members of the Second Church of Woodbridge, believing that the interests of religion require the organization of another church at Metuchen, do hereby mutually agree with each other to enter into the organization of a Protestant Dutch Reformed Church ..."[21]

The 51 signatories consisted of 13 men and 38 women, making up about one-quarter of the membership of the Presbyterian Church. The 13 men included four elders, Stelle Manning, David and Smith Bloomfield, and Albert Edgar, one of whom, Smith Bloomfield, was also President of the Board of Trustees, and another, David Bloomfield, a trustee; William Manning, a trustee, and David Thomas, a deacon. Smith Bloomfield, David Thomas and William Manning were appointed to apply to the Classis of New Brunswick, and the church was formally organized on December 29, 1857, meeting in a house owned by David Thomas. The two Bloomfields, Edgar and Thomas, became elders in the consistory of the new church. William Manning became a deacon in the consistory, along with Martin Compton, Henry Weston, and Charles E. Bloomfield. Some of the participants in this secession may have simply taken advantage of a favorable opportunity to organize a church of a denomination with which they had a closer affinity. Smith Bloomfield and his wife, for instance, joined the Presbyterian Church in 1853 by transfer from the Northwest Protestant Dutch Reformed Church of New York.[22]

Even though the removal of a number of officers of the church left many vacancies to be filled, the two congregations remained on friendly terms. The new Presbyterian minister preached a Thanksgiving Day sermon in 1860 to the combined congregations assembled in the Reformed Church, and in 1865 members of the Session attended the funeral of Smith Bloomfield.[23] It is apparent that the departure of Robert Smith Finley removed the chief irritant to the peace of the community. He left a dual legacy — the Parochial Academy with its concern for the education of youth, and the Reformed Church of Metuchen.

On January 25, 1858, the congregation called to the pulpit Rev. Gardiner Spring Plumley, who was installed by a committee of the Presbytery on April 28, 1858. Rev. Gardiner Spring of Brick Presbyterian Church in New York gave the charge to the pastor. Plumley was a graduate of Yale in 1850 and of Union Theological Seminary in 1855. He preached in New York before coming to Metuchen; his annual salary was set as $700.[24] Like his predecessor, Holloway Whitfield Hunt, whose pastorate was of about the same length, Plumley came to consider Metuchen his home. After leaving Metuchen in 1875, he later became pastor of a Congregational Church in Greenfield Hill, Connecticut; upon his death in 1894 his body was brought to Metuchen for burial in the church's burial ground.[25]

There was a great deal of enthusiasm at the beginning of this pastorate. Plumley was quite popular and his ideas, especially as to the need for increased emphasis upon benevolence, brought some permanent changes in the church. His gentlemanly appearance and polished manners appealed to those who had opposed Finley. This new spirit of unity and dedication enabled the church to recover from the difficulties of the previous years, though unfortunately, controversy eventually arose to mar the last years of Plumley's tenure. Most symbolic of the new spirit was the change in the name of the church. An Act of the State Legislature on February 26, 1858, signed by the Governor on the same day, officially changed its name to the First Presbyterian Church of Metuchen.[26] A revision of the membership roll was carried out later that year and in the annual report to Presbytery, in April 1859, the church reported 136 communicants.[27] That figure was to double before the end of Plumley's pastorate in 1875. The minister organized the work of the church systematically. Session usually met afternoons in the pastor's study four times a year in February, May, August and November, oftener if necessary. Though it continued to exercise discipline over the moral offenses of its members, it ceased to make public announcements of individual cases before the congregation.[28] Regular sessional prayer meetings were held on the first Monday evening of each month.[29]

Plumley's most important contribution to the church was the increased emphasis upon support for benevolences. The Session on May 6, 1858, resolved to take annual collections for the four Boards of the Church, for the Committee of Church Extension, and for the American Bible Society.[30] The collections were taken on the third Sunday of the month; the original schedule set the third Sunday of January for the Board of Foreign Missions, March for the Board of Education, May for the Board of Publication, July for the Board of Domestic Missions, September for the Committee of Church Extension and November for the American Bible Society. Another benevolence was added when the Session decided to take an annual collection on the last Sunday in December for the General Assembly's fund for disabled ministers in need and for needy widows and orphans of deceased ministers. Later, a sum of $300 was raised to support a colporter for one year, for the purpose of distributing religious tracts.[31] It was left to the American Tract Society to decide whether this sum could best be used in the western or southern sections of the country.

The minutes of Session during Plumley's years listed the financial results of these collections that were reported to Presbytery. An examination of these figures shows that, though amounts fluctuated fairly widely from year to year, the Board of Foreign Missions and the Board of Education were the ones most generously supported, with the Board of Publication and the Board of Domestic Missions occupying third and fourth place. The congregation evidently thought least worthy the minister's relief fund. So far as amounts were concerned, over $100 a year for any one fund was substantial support, over $200 very generous.[32] In an effort to increase these collections, the pastor preached an annual sermon on systematic benevolence as a means of grace, and Session established a plan of visiting the members at the time of the annual collections.[33] In 1870, $100 was appropriated from benevolence funds for the support of a theological student.[34]

These sessional statistics also showed the annual collections for congregational purposes, including the minister's salary. For the early years of Plumley's pastorate, they ranged from about $1,200 to about $1,700 annually, and in the later years, with a larger membership, from about $2,200 to about $3,600. Very roughly this averaged out to approximately $10 per person per year. Probably all of these funds were collected in the church services rather than by pew rents. The last record of pew rent collection is for the year ending May 1, 1859, when six collectors took in $844.[35] In 1873 the Session adopted a plan providing for weekly contributions through envelopes to the various objects for which money was required. These included the various Boards and Commissions of the General Assembly, the Sabbath School, the Session Fund, and the Tract Fund.[36]

A continuing problem in the church during these times was the proper use of the Parochial Academy. Plumley did not share Robert Finley's enthusiasm for the education of youth, and in 1859 when the Trustees asked to be allowed to use the building for other purposes, Session granted it, though three elders entered a written protest against the action.[37] Continued correspondence between Session and Trustees revealed some misgivings on the part of Session for their original decision. Plumley apparently felt that the Lecture Room of the Academy should not be used for purely secular purposes, and some members of Session disapproved of the Trustee's practice of renting out the room without referring the applicants to Session for approval.[38] Finally in 1873 the Session drew up a comprehensive policy statement which said that any use of the Lecture Room for purposes inconsistent with the religious character of the Church was injurious to the spiritual interests of the congregation; in particular its use was not approved for "business associations, elections, primary meetings of political parties, or the exhibition of singers or showmen ..."[39] What the spiritual interests of the congregation consisted of may be shown by the fact that permission was given in 1874 to the Y.M.C.A. to sponsor a lecture on Palestine, to the County Temperance Association, and to the ladies of the Methodist Episcopal Church to give a party for their minister.[40] The president of the Y.M.C.A., Judson Gilbert, was also superintendent of the Sunday School.

It is disappointing for the historian to find many statements of Plumley's views about temperance, the need to observe the Sabbath, family responsibility in reading scripture and attending prayer meeting, but none about the great issues raised by the Civil War. The annual pastoral letters that exist do not refer to the war but only to the narrowly religious concerns of the people. Yet there was surely something important for the church to say, especially on the responsibility of the citizen toward the society in which he lived, a sound Puritan concept.

Great crowds greeted Lincoln in February, 1861, as he journeyed by rail from Jersey City to Trenton on the way to his inauguration.[41] But President Lincoln's call for volunteers received only a disappointing response in the township, and the township government began offering bounties from tax money to those who would enlist or get substitutes to fill the township quota. This process proved successful at first, but by 1865 men were being hired from such places as Elizabeth and Clinton to help fill the Woodbridge quota.[42] Undoubtedly there were many volunteers for the Union cause in the Presbyterian Church, but the record appears in marked contrast to the American Revolution.

Dutifully the Church followed the decision by General Assembly to designate July 1, 1861, as a day of special prayer and religious observance "by reason of the present condition of our national affairs ..."[43] An afternoon church service was to be held that day. In September, in accordance with the recommendation of Lincoln, the Church was to observe the last Thursday of the month as a day of fasting, humiliation and prayer.[44] A service was to be held at 10:30 A.M. in the Church, and at 7 P.M. in the Lecture Room. What observances were held in the Church to mark the coming of peace, or to commemorate the assassination of Abraham Lincoln are not recorded.[45] New Jersey contributed much money and many delegates to the work of the United States Christian Commission, which undertook programs of visitation to military camps and hospitals, and the distribution of magazines and books, hymnals and Bibles, to the soldiers. The extent to which First Church may have participated is not known.[46]

The decade from the end of the Civil War to the completion of Plumley's pastorate was marked by considerable growth in both town and church. In the general post-war expansion, Metuchen's role as trading and transportation center became more fully realized. With its chief business area concentrated along the west side of Main Street, Metuchen had blacksmiths, carpenters, country stores, milliners, hotels, a carriage maker, a florist, a flour and grist mill, and a harness maker.[47] Capitalists looking for investment opportunities, began the development of clay deposits near Bonhamtown. Metuchen as a desirable residential area was

The Reverend Azel Roe, D. D. famous pastor of the Revolutionary War era.

The Reverend Adolph H. Behrenberg. Th. D. whose 25th Anniversary coincided with the 250th Anniversary of the congregation.

The Manse, as it appeared in 1898.

The Manse as it appeared originally and as it was later restored.

129

The Church after 1863.

The Church prior to 1958.

The Chapel as it appeared in 1967. Built in 1958.

The Social Center as it appeared in 1967. The cornerstone was laid in 1948.

The Church as renovated in 1958, showing Education Building erected in 1931.

also developing a reputation of having healthful climate, fine landscape, and easy access to large cities.[48] Newly organized activities began to be established. In 1870, a reading room and library were opened under the initiative of the Order of the Sons of Temperance,[49] a foundation both in temperance and in reading on which Rev. James Mason was soon to build. The predecessor of the town's volunteer fire department was Nathan Robins' water brigade, with a runner built by Alexander Ayers, the carriage maker, to carry water buckets, axes, and crowbars; and the forerunner of the police department was a farmers protective organization to combat horse thieves.[50]

Three new churches were founded in Metuchen in the immediate post-war years, to confirm the growth that had started with the Reformed Church in 1857. In 1866 St. Luke's Episcopal Church was established; until 1869 it used the Reformed Church for its services. The Centenary Methodist Episcopal Church was also established in 1866, and in similar fashion used the Academy of the Presbyterian Church until its own was built in 1869.[51] Finally in 1870 St. Francis Roman Catholic Church was founded, serving a wide area of the region.[52]

The growing activity and increasing population brought new people into the church in increasing numbers in the post-war years. From 1866 to 1872 the membership of the Presbyterian Church grew from 174 to 273, with 1868 being the greatest single year of growth; 68 were admitted in that year, 48 in the month of February alone. In the years after 1872, it declined somewhat, as other ministers in the area proved more appealing than Plumley.[53] His last annual report, in 1875, recorded 232 members. New names appear: Hartenstein, Hopkins, Hanschild, Knapp, Melick, Weed, Blackford, Doolittle, Coddington, Long. From the Record of Baptisms kept by Plumley, which listed the father's occupation, it is possible to see the changing character of the church's membership. Farmers still predominate, but they by no means monopolize occupation as they once did. Among the parents of those baptized by Plumley were listed the following: State Senator, U.S. collector, surgeon, grocer, real estate salesman, railroad clerk, horticulturalist, carpenter, merchant, station agent, laborer, draftsman, physician, sea master. Rev. Mason, who kept up this information until 1883, listed in addition: machinist, mechanic, undertaker, saddler, telephone operator; in the 1880s as before, however, farming was the most common occupation indicated.[54] Nothing so clearly indicates that church and town were changing in nature even as they were growing in size. After 1875, however, Presbyterianism in general was to find itself less attractive than other denominations to the new immigrants and the new industrialized working class.

Increasing mobility was likewise a characteristic of the population, as people moved out of the area as well as in. Plumley in 17 years admitted a total of 326 new members. One of his predecessors, Hunt, admitted 198 in 19 years, and Henry Cook, in 30 years, admitted 257. Both Cook's and Plumley's times were characterized by increasing net membership, but the overall rate of admission was twice as high in the latter period. A constantly changing membership, so characteristic of the present church, was already beginning to appear a century ago.

The physical appearance of the church was altered in 1863 with the addition of a steeple, and a church bell in 1865.[55] A small pipe organ, previously used in the Institute for the Blind in New York, was purchased and installed in 1871, and in the same year the church was equipped with a coal furnace.[56] Judson H. Gilbert was appointed organist and director of music; two years later he also became the superintendent of the Sunday School.[57] Gilbert's assistant, David T. Marshall, played the organ during choir practice. In his Reminiscences, Marshall recalled one Sunday noon when there was a fire at Mr. Yingling's house on Rector Place. As he was "blowing" the organ at the end of the service he heard the church bell "ringing the long roll" which meant fire; he left quickly so he wouldn't be held up to play for choir practice.[58]

Rev. Plumley wrote a pastoral letter each year which was a brief annual report of his activities. The letter of January 1, 1870, illustrates well the activities of the church. Plumley reported that in his twelve years as pastor up to that time he had made 4,378 pastoral visits, baptized 127 individuals, conducted 227 funerals, solemnized 83 marriages, and admitted 230 new members.[59] Divine worship was now held in the church each Sunday morning and evening. There was a Sabbath School on Sunday afternoon, and a prayer meeting each Wednesday evening in the Lecture Room of the Academy. The pastor spoke of resuming "female prayer meetings" in his Study on Thursday afternoons. He emphasized the need for the church to furnish its youth with instruction and recreation, especially in the light of increased building activity in the town. "If ... a proper effort is made, they will doubtless not only be drawn from the haunts of dissipation, but become established in the habit of totally abstaining from all intoxicating drinks." The pastor called upon the people to follow in Jesus' steps in their lives. "We live in days when objects of mere worldly interest are pursued with unwonted activity and zeal. In the race for the golden prize of riches, all the energies of body, mind and soul seem employed ..."

The final years of Plumley's pastorate were marked by controversy. On June 11, 1873, Plumley first gave notice that he would request Presbytery to dissolve the pastoral relation.[60] The Presbytery, noting that the pastor had said in his request that there were some in the congregation who wanted this dissolution, asked representatives of the congregation to appear at a Presbytery meeting to show cause why the request should not be granted.[61] At that meeting, the commissioners presented a resolution, adopted by a vote of 45-20, that the congregation did not concur with the pastor's request, and Presbytery accordingly decided not to allow Plumley to resign.[62] That there was strong feeling against Plumley, however, was shown by the immediate resignation of two elders, John Watson and John Voorhees, and of A. W. Marshall, the Sunday School superintendent.[63] In addition, many of those who wanted him to leave began deliberately to absent themselves from worship services, and petitioned Presbytery to dissolve the pastoral relation.[64] Plumley took these defections seriously. First he deliberately installed three new elders directly from the congregation, without previous nomination, only one day after the resignation of the other two.[65] Then he undertook to bring the discipline of the church against those who continued to be willfully absent from church services. This effort was unsuccessful, however; many were simply attending other churches.

In 1875 Presbytery undertook to determine for itself whether or not the congregation wanted to retain Plumley. Its investigation showed a decided majority in favor of keeping him, and accordingly it reaffirmed its earlier decision and decided not to allow a dissolution.[66] The dispute was not satisfactorily resolved, however, and Plumley finally resigned his pastorate in December, 1875.

In its resolution marking the resignation, Session spoke of his faithful performance of pastoral duties, his gentlemanly Christian character, and his kindness and courtesy. "We deeply regret the dissolution ... which has for eighteen years been ... so highly conducive to the prosperity of the church."[67] Though rather narrow in his outlook and his conception of Christian responsibility, he had succeeded in bringing the church through a period of growth and vitality at a time when there were many other interests competing for the attention of the people.

During the early months of 1876, the pulpit was filled by Rev. John F. Pingry, appointed as supply by Presbytery. A congregation meeting on March 22, 1876, elected four new elders, Augustus Blackford, William Martin, John Clarkson and Francis Grimstead.[68] Other ministers who preached and acted as Moderators of Session during 1876 included Rev. David A. Cunningham of Philadelphia, Rev. Peter H. Brooks of Susquehanna, Pennsylvania, and Rev. Samuel H. Kellogg. A committee was appointed in April to seek a permanent minister; in September a congregation meeting extended a unanimous call to Rev. Samuel D. Burchard of New York, but he declined the call.[69]

Rev. James G. Mason of Washington, D. C., supplied the pulpit on the first two Sundays of January, 1877. At a congregation meeting on January 23 the congregation called Mason to the pulpit, offering a salary of $1,200. Mason immediately accepted and was installed by the Presbytery on April 24, 1877.[70] For almost half a century, until 1925, his life and the life of the church were to be one.

Chapter XIII

STATISTICS

Finley
> *Marriages* — 34
> *Baptisms* — 70
> *Total Admissions* — 67

Plumley
> *Marriages* — 83 (to January 1, 1870 only)
> *Baptisms* — 168
> *Total Admissions* — 326

CHAPTER XIII — FOOTNOTES

1. Ezra Hunt, *History of the Churches of Metuchen,* New York 1870, 16. Wallace N. Jamison, *Religion in New Jersey: A Brief History,* Princeton 1964, 100.
2. William H. Ayers, *A History of the First Presbyterian Church of Metuchen,* Metuchen, New Jersey 1947, 23-4.
3. William Starr Myers, ed., *The Story of New Jersey,* New York 1945, II, 304-5, 328-9.
4. Hunt, *op. cit.,* 16; J. Lloyd Grimstead manuscript on The First Presbyterian Church, p. 9. The Academy was located on the north side of Amboy Avenue opposite Graham Avenue.
5. *Metuchen, The Brainy Borough,* unpublished, (hereafter referred to as Library Manuscript), ch. 10, p. 7.
6. J. Lloyd Grimstead miscellaneous notes, p. 6.
7. Library Manuscript, *op. cit.,* ch. 10, p. 8; David T. Marshall, *Recollections of Boyhood Days in Old Metuchen,* New York 1929, 41. In Metuchen the only public school in the 19th century was the Franklin School. Education there was free, i.e., tax-supported, hence tuition free, by state law beginning in 1861.
8. Session minutes, May 28, 1853.
9. Ayers, *op. cit.,* 24. Whether the pastor was opposed to festival money in principle or because of objectionable behavior by individuals is not clear.
10. Session minutes, December 29, 1856.
11. Session minutes, December 29, 1856, January 5, February 13, 1857.
12. Session minutes, April 20, May 7, 1857.
13. Session minutes, July 31, September 3, 1857.
14. Letter, dated August 12, 1857, appeared in the *Weekly Fredonian,* August 28, 1857; copy in miscellaneous notes of J. Lloyd Grimstead.
15. Letter, dated November 30, 1857, appeared in *Weekly Fredonian,* December 4, 1857; copy in miscellaneous notes of J. Lloyd Grimstead.
16. Session minutes, September 3, 1857. Both had resigned as elders at the time of the dispute concerning Holloway Whitfield Hunt.
17. Session minutes, September 14, 15 and 21, 1857. The testimony in Campbell's hearing is not included in the minutes, but stated simply as being "on file".

18. Session minutes, October 3, 1857.

19. Text of this resolution taken from letter cited in previous footnote #15.

20. Session minutes, November 7, 1857.

21. Rev. Harry VerStrate, *The Reformed Church of Metuchen,* Metuchen, New Jersey 1957 (pages unnumbered). The Session granted certificates of dismissal to 31 on November 27, 1857, and to 10 more in December and the following February.

22. Session minutes, May 7, 1853.

23. Library manuscript, *op. cit.,* ch. 11, p. 6; Session minutes, May 12, 1865. The new Reformed Church was dedicated August 5, 1858.

24. Hunt, *History of the Churches of Metuchen, op. cit.,* 17; Session minutes, new series, vol. I, p. 1-3.

25. Ayers, *op. cit.,* 24. For Plumley's character, see the approving letter of "Veritas," an anti-Finley correspondent of the *Weekly Fredonian,* January 29, 1858; in miscellaneous notes of J. Lloyd Grimstead.

26. Session minutes, new series, vol. I, 2-3.

27. Session minutes, December 6, 1858; April 11, 1859.

28. Session minutes, June 9, July 7, 1860; Library manuscript, *op. cit.,* ch. 11, p. 5.

29. Session minutes, August 7, 1858.

30. Session minutes, May 8, June 1, 1858. The schedule was slightly revised from time to time.

31. Session minutes February 5, August 6, 1867.

32. Analysis of Session minutes showing statistics of report to Presbytery for various years. There were isolated instances of larger amounts.

33. Session minutes, August 10, 1864.

34. Session minutes, February 8, 1870.

35. Book containing copies of the lists of Pew rent to be collected by the Trustees. In Session minutes there are occasionally references to pewholders.

36. Session minutes, December 1, 1873.

37. Session minutes, May 7, October 1, 1859. The three protesters were Ezra Hunt, William Ross and John Watson.

38. Session minutes, December 22, 1873. Prayer meetings on Sunday evening and Wednesday evening were held there.

39. Session minutes, February 24, 1873.

40. Session minutes, January 21, March 28, 1874.

41. Earl S. Miers, ed., *New Jersey and the Civil War,* Princeton 1964, 1-7.

42. Library manuscript, *op. cit.,* ch. 2, p. 7-8. The picture in the state as a whole was apparently considerably better than in the township. But the newspaper press was divided in its views. See Miers, *op. cit.,* 21, 26, 36, 109-111.

43. Session minutes, June 26, 1861.

44. Session minutes, September 13, 1861.

45. His funeral train passed through Metuchen, again drawing large crowds to witness its tragic journey. See Miers, *op. cit.,* 130-1.

46. Jamison, *op. cit.,* 107-8.

47. Library manuscript, ch. 7, p. 7-8. Business grew at Holly Street when a new railroad station was built there in 1875 to replace the Main Street station, destroyed by fire in 1870.

48. Hunt, *Metuchen and Her History, op. cit.,* 26. When Raritan Township was formed in 1870, Metuchen was its natural center. An occasional township meeting was held in one of Metuchen's hotels. See Library manuscript, *op. cit.,* ch. 2, p. 9.

49. *Ibid.;* Library manuscript, ch. 9, p. 5.

50. Library manuscript, *op. cit.,* ch. on Fire Department, p. 1; ch. on Police Department, p. 3.

51. Hunt, *History of the Churches of Metuchen, op. cit.,* 20-1; Library manuscript, ch. 11, p. 11.

52. Catholics in the South Plainfield area came to church via hand car on the Lehigh Valley railroad. See New Brunswick *Sunday Home News,* June 21, 1964. Section A.

53. These figures are taken from the annual reports to Presbytery, contained in Session minutes. Evidence of dissatisfaction with Plumley can be seen in Session's action, April 25, 1874, in citing 19 persons for chronic absence from church, two for publicly criticizing the pastor, and two for unlawfully organizing a meeting to secure his removal. A long and detailing questioning of each of the accused is included in the minutes of Session.

54. Information taken from Register of Baptisms, mostly in the 1870s and 1880s.
55. Hunt, *History of the Churches of Metuchen, op. cit.,* 17.

56. Mason, *op. cit.,* 69; Ayers, *op. cit.,* 25.

57. Session minutes, February 11, 1871.
58. David T. Marshall, *Recollections of Boyhood Days in Old Metuchen,* New York 1929, 124.
59. Pastor's Annual Letter, January 1, 1870.
60. Session minutes, June 11, 1873.
61. Session minutes, October 20, 1873.
62. Session minutes, recording the meeting of Presbytery on November 4, 1873.
63. Session minutes, November 8, December 1, 1873.
64. Session minutes, April 25, 1874.
65. Session minutes, November 8 and 9, 1873; February 26, 1875 recording statement of Rev. John Swing of Elizabeth Presbytery.
66. Session minutes April 30, 1875; minutes of Presbytery, June 15, 1875.
67. Session minutes, December 11, 1875.
68. Session minutes, March 11, 1876.
69. Session minutes, April 8, 1876; minutes of congregation meeting, September 21, 1876.
70. Historical statement in Session minutes.

Chapter XIV

MASON: THE FIRST TWENTY-FIVE YEARS

"... his baptisms of approximately five hundred into the Christian faith and reception of over eight hundred into the fellowship of this church, have left their marks upon us as indelibly as the marks of the doors ... upon the entrances of the pews of our old and historic church ..."
– Session minutes, June 1, 1938

"It is possible to satisfy our conscience by the gift of a crust to every tramp that comes to our door. But God delights to hear a more virile song than that. As Christ brake the loaves and distributed them, so must we brake ourselves and distribute our good doing, through the widest circle of the world ... as Christians and as citizens we must live the unselfish life."
– Thanksgiving sermon, 1891

"The old Presbyterian bell had a very sweet, low tone."
– David T. Marshall, Recollections of Boyhood Days in Old Metuchen

$\mathbf{W}$ITHOUT A DOUBT, James Gilbert Mason was the most illustrious minister who served the Metuchen church. His pastorate extended over 48 years, from January 1877 to June 1925, a period of time which witnessed, up to the first World War, the high tide of vigor, prosperity and social influence of Protestantism, all of which were strongly reflected in the leadership and activity of the Metuchen church. Mason was a well known pastor in an age of great preachers, and his emphasis on benevolence and mission work was typical of Protestant efforts of the time. The late years of his service came at a time when the influence of Protestantism was declining sharply in the post-war years.

But Mason's field of influence and interest was wider than his pulpit and his church. He took a strong and direct interest in the affairs of Metuchen itself, helping to found its library and to foster its intellectual life, helping to reduce the influence of its saloons and defend the sanctity of the Sabbath, writing letters to the newspapers to take a stand on a great variety of questions and issues, and indeed supporting the movement which led to the organization of the Borough of Metuchen in 1900.

The wider community attracted him too, both through the church and through his interest in public questions. He played a prominent role in the General Assembly of the Presbyterian Church, to which he was six times a commissioner. There he defended the liberal forces against the orthodox in the developing theology of the time, and he was a candidate for moderator at the 1891 General Assembly where the theological dispute reached its climax.

Mason saw no reason why he should not take an active part in the political affairs of his state and nation. A Republican until the Bull Moose split in 1912, he subsequently became a leading figure in the Prohibition party, and tried hard, though never with success, to achieve public office. Dignified and aristocratic in appearance, powerful and direct in speech, clear and definite in the position he took on any question, Mason left an indelible mark upon the church to which he devoted his life work.

144

A native of Jonesboro, Tennessee, Mason graduated from Williams College in 1863 and from Union Theological Seminary in 1866. While a student at the Seminary, he served with the United States Sanitary Commission during the Civil War. Part of this time he preached in a mission at Woodhaven, Long Island, and after his ordination by the Presbytery of New York on July 4, 1866, he returned to Woodhaven to found a church and to become its first pastor. In 1867 he returned to Tennessee to serve the church in his home town for five years, after which he was called to the pulpit of North Presbyterian Church in Washington, D. C. At the beginning of that pastorate he married Sue Tyler of Virginia; her untimely death in 1876 caused Mason to resign his charge, and during the next year he travelled abroad to Europe and the Holy Land. Upon his return he preached in the Metuchen church in January 1877, and then accepted the call to Metuchen over ones to Baltimore and to Sedalia, Missouri. He was officially installed as pastor of First Presbyterian Church on April 24, 1877.[1]

Protestantism in the United States reached the peak of its influence during the years between 1875 and the end of the first World War. Larger and more substantial churches were built, more decorative in style. In an age when oratory as an art carried great prestige, individual clergymen gained reputations that sometimes extended far beyond their own churches and communities. At the same time, laymen began to play an increasingly significant role in Protestant activities. Great efforts were made to organize and improve the Sunday School curriculum. The church, becoming more of a social institution, put greater emphasis on the social, recreational and educational services it might render to its parishioners and to its community. But changes in society, especially the growing urbanism of American life and the new tide of immigrants, were presenting challenges to Protestantism that it proved difficult to meet successfully.[2] The long established Puritan Sabbath was being challenged by Catholic tradition and the customs of new nationality groups, and increasing numbers of working men did not find Protestant churches, and especially Presbyterian ones, the answer to their own needs.[3]

To meet these varied challenges, new organizations were founded, both within and without the church, to become "instruments of Protestant action." The Christian Endeavor Society was organized in 1881 and spread rapidly in the next years.[4] Major efforts to reaffirm the value of temperance led to the founding of the Women's Christian Temperance Union in 1873, with primary emphasis on temperance education in schools, and the Anti-Saloon League in 1895 with its emphasis on political activity to establish prohibition.[5]

In similar fashion, traditional ideas of theology were under attack, not only as a result of changes in American life but also as a result of the intellectual influence of Charles Darwin and the development of Biblical higher criticism. The New Theology began to support currents of secular thought that emphasized man's liberty instead of his depravity, and the possibility of his moral improvement, supported by God's love, more than his sinful nature. There developed an optimistic view of man's destiny which could achieve the kingdom of God through dedicated service to social improvement. The gospel of wealth acquired theological support through such works as Russell Conwell's *Acres of Diamonds*.[6] Finally, there were efforts at development of the social gospel, the Christian concern for the evils of society and the need for social reform.[7] This aspect was opposed on the one hand by big business enterprise, and on the other by the evangelical emphasis on individual behavior, represented in this age by Dwight Moody.

The activity of James G. Mason and his church both reflected and contributed to these broad developments. Mason's many civic projects, his political interests, his concern for his congregation and for the church, and his intellectual leadership were all important facets of the vital role that he played in the life of his church, his town, and his nation.

At the beginning of Mason's pastorate the church numbered about 200 members. The Session, the Sabbath School and the Women's Foreign

Missionary Society were its important active bodies.[8] The per capita annual subscription for the support of the church was just over $18, and for benevolence $1.27. Besides the Sunday service, there was a Wednesday evening prayer meeting, and a ladies' meeting on Thursday. Communion occurred four times a year, in March, June, September and December. Friday evening prayer meetings led by elders were instituted in 1878 and held in school houses "in the outposts of the congregation,"[9] probably at New Durham, Bonhamtown, Oak Tree, and Menlo Park.[10]

The manse was a busy place in Mason's early years. John Marshall conducted a private school in the west end of the parsonage. In 1878 about 30 were on the roll, including four members of Marshall's family.[11] For a time Marshall's large family lived at the parsonage.[12] On April 4, 1881, Mason married Anita Hauschild and their two children, Irene and Gilbert, were born and brought up in the manse. The children and their playmates used the old wing as a playroom, and sometimes "camped out" there on Saturdays. Flowers, vegetable gardens and fruit trees were all around. A locust grove stood west of the manse, and a large cherry tree was just outside Irene's window.[13] There were summer tennis parties followed by cold raspberry punch. In the winter tobogganing on Daniels Hill (Hillside Avenue) was a favorite sport. A large birthday party planned for Irene on March 12, 1888, was never held because the guests could not get through the great blizzard. The food that had been prepared for the party was not wasted, however. When a railroad train became stalled in a snowdrift near the manse, the men of the community took the chicken salad, birthday cake and some hot coffee to feed the hungry passengers. Amid all the bustle of activity in these years, Reverend Mason carried on his pastoral calling with a horse and buggy the children called the Gospel Car.

From the very beginning of his pastorate, Mason stressed the need to improve giving by his congregation. An envelope system was begun in 1877 to encourage more widespread and more systematic giving.[14]

Mason took many opportunities to emphasize to his congregation the need to support both the activities of the local church and through benevolence, the mission field that stretched without limit to any part of the country and beyond. He was able to report in 1879 that the debt existing at the beginning of his pastorate was now almost paid up.[15] His emphasis was always spiritual and he gave many sermons on tithing. In his Sessional Letter of January 1, 1890, he asked for systematic giving in support of the church. "The Trustees and Session may speak of this by authority, but I speak as your Pastor, persuasively, knowing that it is for your spiritual good."

Mission work was of great interest to this generation of Christians. It sometimes came out in incidental and almost frivolous ways, to help in any cause. In 1885 Session ordered a special collection to contribute toward an endowment fund to establish a German Theological School at Bloomfield, N. J.[16] In 1905 an Easter Sunday collection was taken for the benefit of the building fund of the Magyar Church of Perth Amboy.[17] The Session meeting of April 9, 1895, recorded, "A balance of $4.79 was reported from the Anti-Race Track Fund, and it was decided to send the money to help relieve the suffering farmers in Nebraska." That same year a balance of $12.98 in the Deacons Fund was turned over to the Sunday School treasurer to buy temperance books for the Sunday School library.

More systematic efforts were more fruitful in their results. The Young Ladies Home Missionary Society was organized at a meeting called by the pastor on October 3, 1879. Obeying the command, "go ye into the world and preach the gospel to every creature," the young women emphasized their goal to develop interest in home missions and engage in home missions work. The group made clothing and other materials to send to schools and missions in various parts of the country. In 1880 a box with aprons, mittens and underclothing, all made by the members, was sent to a school in Utah. The next year, bedding, clothing and copies of the New Testament were contributed.[18] Over the years, money raised by the society was sent as a contribution to the salaries of teachers in Utah, Tennessee, North Carolina, New Mexico, and South Dakota. Cutting and sewing carpet rags, making garments from muslin, holding informal social affairs to raise a little money in addition to the regular dues of five cents a month, constituted the general activity. Finances were difficult at first, but after the early years, the society was able to contribute about $100 a year to these causes. Occasionally, donations were made closer to home. The meeting of December 15, 1880, for instance, was given over to work to provide some local poor children with suitable clothing so that they might attend Sabbath School during the winter. Miss Susie McFarland was the first president, and for a time in the 1880s the pastor's wife served in that capacity. About 20 women constituted the active membership; eventually the group was merged into the Foreign Missionary Society.[19]

The Ladies Aid Society, founded in 1888 "to promote an earnest Christian working life among its members," was a more formal organization than the Home Missionary Society. It met more often, observed all the parliamentary proceedings of minutes and committee reports, and had a larger attendance and a richer treasury. Its main effort was to raise funds to meet the needs of the local church. It maintained six committees: executive, finance, purchasing, cutting, visiting, and entertainment; much of its meeting time was taken up with sewing and quilting.[20] In 1889 and 1890 at the request of the Trustees it helped to raise money for a new roof and new lamps for the church; in 1894 it paid off a coal bill and in 1899 bought a new carpet. Over a long period of years the Ladies Aid Society helped to pay the salary of an organist and raise funds for the music committee, and it contributed a share of the church sexton's salary.

Its money raising activities were various and usually successful. A traditional one was an annual Strawberry and Ice Cream Festival in June. A cook book committee raised $200, a lawn festival at Mrs. Campbell's home in 1890 brought in almost $40 profit, and a church fair and supper

149

in October 1891 cleared $157. The coal bill during the winter of 1893-4 was paid for through the Society's sponsorship of a musical program, and an early spring supper in the social room; the charge for the latter was 25 cents, with salad and ice cream extra. A Sunbonnet Drill in the fall of 1894 raised over $50. In 1897 the Society purchased several dozen cups, saucers and plates for the use of different groups in the church. On the Masons' wedding anniversary in 1898, the Society presented a table-cloth and a dozen napkins to Mrs. Mason. The statement of Alice Mundy, secretary, at the end of the Society's annual report in March 1901, well expressed the attitude and diligence of the ladies of the aid.

> The work done by the Aid Society is of an unostentatious char-acter and does not proclaim itself to the world, yet we are constrained to believe that its work, earnestly continued from year to year, must aggregate a great deal of good which will only be known at the final recording day.

A variety of changes and improvements to the church buildings came during the 1880s. In 1883 the Academy building was moved from its location northwest of the church to a position adjoining the church on its west side.[21] Its rooms were used for the Sunday School and for various social meetings. Kerosene lamps in front of the church and in front of the parsonage were installed and maintained by the Village Improvement Society.[22] In 1888 stained glass windows were installed in the church.[23] The sale of a strip of land to the rear of the church and along the cemetery to the Pennsylvania Railroad to build a new station helped to pay for this improvement.[24]

It was in these years, too, that the church bell had to be repaired. As a boy, David Marshall had the job of ringing the church bell. The custom was to ring four strokes, wait a minute, and ring four more. The bell, which had a "very sweet, low tone," cracked in 1890 and had to be sent to Troy, N. Y., for recasting.[25] The bell served as the village fire alarm too, ringing the long roll to alert the firemen, whose equipment for a time was housed in a brick firehouse on land the church subsequently sold to the railroad.[26]

James Mason always tried to maintain good relations with his congregation and avoid any outbreak of dissension. In 1882 a brief argument did occur, however, which led Mason to submit his resignation. According to a news clipping in Mrs. Harper's scrapbook, the reasons for Mason's resignation included his fruitless attempt "to unite the two branches of the Presbyterian Church in this place." Apparently a few members of the congregation wanted to organize or join an independent church belonging to a southern Presbyterian Assembly, and Mason's insistence on union in the face of this partisanship led to his offer of resignation. The congregation, by ballot, refused to accept his resignation, and no further incidents of this kind occurred.

Other than this brief flurry, Mason's relations with the congregation were very good in these years. In 1881 the Session rescinded a rule, in effect for about five years, providing for the rotation of elders by making them ineligible for reelection until after one year had elapsed from the expiration of their term. The effect of this action was to keep existing elders in office for many years, sometimes decades, until voluntary resignation or death removed them from office. As Session became more deeply involved in supervising the activities of the church, its earlier function of disciplining individual members for their conduct gradually became less important. Occasional cases did appear. One parishioner was disciplined for stealing; a woman was disciplined for frequent intoxication, keeping open her store on the Lord's Day, and being absent four years from church services. Suspension from the church for a term was sometimes publicly announced.[27]

During the 1880s Mason was already beginning to take a prominent role in the affairs of Metuchen and the surrounding area. Thomas A. Edison was a close friend of Mason. One of the earliest public exhibitions of Edison's phonograph occurred in the Presbyterian Church before a capacity crowd that had come to enjoy the entertainment.[28]

151

Mason did much to encourage the intellectual activities which were becoming prominent in Metuchen in these years. Writers, editors, artists and others of similar bent were giving Metuchen the early foundation of its reputation as a "brainy borough." Henry Mills Alden, editor of Harpers Magazine until early in the 20th century, had been a friend of Mason at Williams College. In 1868 he became a resident of Metuchen and helped to found its library.[29] Mrs. Hester M. Poole, a poet, literary critic and feminist, founded the Quiet Hour in 1895, for discussions on literature, social matters and feminism.[30] Mary Wilkins Freeman, short story writer, lived in Metuchen in the early years of the 20th century. Mason's interests fitted in well with these activities. In 1879 he had formed a literary and debating society. This experiment proved unsuccessful at first when the members could not resolve the problem of admitting women, but the society was revived at a later time.[31] More lasting was Mason's activity as a member of a committee of the Village Improvement Society, appointed to establish a library in Metuchen. As a result, the Village Reading Room and Library Association was formed in 1884 at a meeting held in the social room of the Presbyterian Church.[32] The next year the association was given a room at the Franklin School. Private funds, including an important legacy from Theodore Hunt, professor of literature at Princeton and son of Ezra Hunt, aided the future growth of the library, including the construction of its first building at Robins Place and Hillside Avenue.

If Mason involved himself in efforts to improve the intellectual life of the citizens, he also was passionately concerned about keeping their minds free from the influence of alcohol. Temperance was one of Mason's guiding principles, and it was eventually to lead him into long and concerted political activity. Before that occurred, however, Mason had supported the organization of a Temperance Society in 1884 drawn from members of the Sabbath School.[33] He convinced the church to support his endeavors, and in 1890 the Session sent four delegates, A. W. Marshall,

J. H. Gilbert, R. B. Crowell, and Mason, to the National Temperance Conference in New York.[34]

Mason's interests in all of these community concerns were frequently reflected in his sermons. Beyond the themes related to theology, the prosperity of the church, and its mission outreach through benevolence, Mason thought that the church had an obligation to give guidance on civic affairs, and to make people aware of the church's relation to world events, and the people's obligations as Christians.[35] A good example of this emphasis was Mason's Thanksgiving sermon in 1891, preached on the text in Matthew 15:36-8, the parable of the loaves and fishes.[36] He spoke of Christ's ability to transform the little into the great, and his ability to distribute his gifts (he brake the bread). It was not enough to acknowledge God's gifts and to speak our thanks for them. It was our obligation to support worthy causes.

> It is praiseful of God if we advocate any good cause, if we help onward any beneficent work ... Let us not minimize our obligated manifestations of gratitude to the easy good kindheartedness which a weak sentimentalism suggests. It is possible to satisfy our conscience by the gift of a crust to every tramp that comes to our door. But God delights to hear a more virile song than that. As Christ brake the loaves and distributed them, so must we brake ourselves and distribute our good doing, through the widest circle of the world — in the home, in the church, in the village, in the state, in the nation; as Christians and as citizens we must live the unselfish life.

This was Reverend James Gilbert Mason, 14 years pastor of a church which had reached a temporary peak of 300 members, a man who practiced what he preached, and who now became in 1891 a delegate to the 103rd General Assembly, and an active candidate for its leadership as moderator.

The meeting of the General Assembly in the spring of 1891 was held at the Fort Street Presbyterian Church in Detroit, Michigan. Mason was one of four delegates prominently mentioned for moderator, and he was generally regarded as independent of any particular faction within the assembly. Mason was characterized "as a representative young man in the active pastorate ... a representative also of the progressive conservatism of our church ... a man of Southern birth and Northern adoption ..."[37] Though he had many supporters for the office of moderator, Mason was not the overall favorite, and gave way gracefully to a more prominent candidate from New Jersey, Professor William H. Green of Princeton Theological Seminary, who was elected moderator.

The major issue at the Assembly, which was to have repercussions far into the future, arose from contradictory interpretations of a speech made early in the year by Professor Charles Briggs, upon his appointment to a new chair of Biblical Theology at Union Theological Seminary. Briggs' address was sympathetic to the newer, more liberal trends in religious thought which were becoming current. He emphasized the validity of the new historical and textual criticism of the Bible based on reason. To his critics he was directly challenging the inerrancy of Scripture that was a part of the Westminster Confession. Briggs discussion of redemption, and his willingness to support rationalism also were regarded as potentially dangerous. The Presbytery of New York preferred charges of heresy against him. A resolution introduced into the Assembly disapproving of Briggs' appointment led to an acrimonious two-day debate, in which the issue of freedom of investigation versus orthodoxy was sometimes lost in accusations that this was really a battle between conservative orthodox theology of Princeton, which dominated the Assembly, and the efforts of Union and New York to overthrow that predominance.

Mason's views on this controversy leaned toward support of Briggs,[38] but were more moderate than the views of the partisan leaders on either side. Mason wrote letters to the press, giving his opinion that Briggs should not be judged hastily, that there was need for freedom of thought in religious matters, and that, though Briggs differed with the Westminster Confession in some respects, they were not so serious as to justify the charge of heresy. His views were reported to have "created a favorable ripple" among the assembled clergymen. One observer editorialized, "Dr. Mason is not an old fogy or a dangerous radical.... He lives in Metuchen ... 26 miles from Princeton and the same distance from Union Theological School in New York City, and this illustrates very fairly his position with regard to the contending factions in the two institutions."[39]

The report of an Assembly committee vetoing Briggs' appointment was adopted by the Assembly by a vote of 446-60. Mason was one of the 60 who were recorded in opposition to the action. Briggs' eventual suspension from the ministry led thereafter to Union Seminary's withdrawal from Presbyterian control, and helped to lay the basis for the modernist-fundamentalist controversy in the 20th century.[40] The whole matter suggests that Mason was not rigid and dogmatic in his theology, but willing to entertain and test new ideas and new approaches. In an era that stressed denominationalism he found more significance in reducing factional differences, an interest that even bridged different religious groups. According to his daughter, one of Mason's best friends in Metuchen was a Catholic priest, with whom he enjoyed many conversations over religious matters.[41]

On matters that he considered important, Mason was always willing to jump into the middle of any controversy. Mason's opposition to the liquor traffic embroiled him in controversy with Judge Woodbridge Strong of the Court of Common Pleas of Middlesex County over the licensing of a second hotel in Metuchen in 1897.[42] Mason's appearance in court to oppose the applicants brought a criticism from the Judge that Mason was trying to dictate to the court, and the lawyer for the applicants remarked that members of the cloth should save souls and not run the politics of the country. Mason lost his court battle, but ten days later a mass meeting

155

held in the Presbyterian Church unanimously upheld Mason and criticized the Judge for reprimanding a citizen who was critical of its procedures. A card with the initials TWH (Theodore Hunt?) was circulated proclaiming "Hurrah for the John Knox of Middlesex County." The controversy attracted the interest of some New York newspapers, whose editorials were generally favorable to Mason.

In another example of this kind of activity, a meeting was held at the Presbyterian Church in 1904, with many speakers, to protest the state's race track bills. Mason wrote a letter to the New Brunswick Home News praising ministers who had denounced those bills from the pulpit; another letter about the same time protested the action of the Freeholders in holding a pigeon shoot.[43]

Of course not all such activities were in protest. Mason supported the efforts of local citizens to establish a borough separate from Raritan Township. The citizens' meeting in Robins Hall on January 8, 1900 voted in favor of the incorporation of a separate borough by a vote of 73-50.[44] Apparently the reason for the move was a new township law enlarging the powers of its committees and the resulting fear that Metuchen might lose its new street lighting system just established in 1899, and possibly even its new fire department, organized in 1897. Before the vote was taken, there was lively discussion over whether or not it would be possible to find a mayor and six councilmen who would serve without pay, and over whether the town would have sufficient tax revenue to provide needed services. There were always the skeptics of change. Cyrus Poole remarked, "It is nonsense to establish a government over frogs and frog ponds."

Meanwhile, the church's activities continued to develop and additions and changes took place in the physical plant. A brief revival conducted by an evangelist in 1894 brought in 55 new members in late February and early March, and by April 1 the annual report to Presbytery showed 331 members, a significant increase from the 275 of the previous year.[45] This increase did not last, however, as subsequent annual reports in the three following years showed 278, 273 and 262 members respectively. It is a fact that the church's membership increased only very modestly over the long tenure of this ministry, from 200 in 1877 to 308 in 1925. Only 431 new members were received in the first 25 years, an average of about 17 a year.[46] In addition, many of those who joined bore the traditional family names that had always been at the heart of the church. Among the 55 who joined in the 1894 revival can be found the following family names: Bloomfield, Thornall, Mundy, Campbell, Compton, Crowell, Martin, Ayers, Freeman, Tappan. Nothing could better illustrate that the Metuchen Presbyterian Church was not reaching very far beyond its original scope in attracting new members from the growing and changing population of the area, with New Yorkers becoming suburbanites and Italian and Irish immigrant families arriving in large numbers.

A house was built for the sexton in 1895 for somewhat less than $3,000, and in 1898 the one-room school house was removed from the west end of the parsonage and a bay window and broad piazza built for just over $300.[47] On the night of February 28, 1899, a chandelier of kerosene lamps fell in the interior of the church and started a fire. Quick response of the fire companies fortunately saved the building from major damage. Session expressed its thanks to the firemen and soon took steps to authorize the installation of electric lights.[48]

In July 1895 Mason requested Session to grant him four months' leave of absence plus two months' vacation time to go to Europe with his family.[49] The leave was granted and the family was away from Metuchen from September 1895 to February 1896. During at least part of that time Rev. David Stevenson acted as supply. Upon the family's return a series of illustrated talks were scheduled by the pastor. A large poster advertising the series was entitled "Views of the Old World Through the Stereopticon."[50] Three evening lectures were scheduled in May and June 1896, the first on London, Holland and Belgium; the second on Switzerland

157

and Italy; the third on Germany. Irene spoke on A Visit to the Home of Shakespeare; Ramblings of an American Girl Amid the Ruins of Ancient Rome; and Potsdam, the Palace of Frederick the Great. Gilbert talked on St. Ursula, Church of the Bones at Cologne; The Ascent of Mount Blanc; How We Climbed Mount Vesuvius — The Trained Fleas at Florence; and the House of Luther at Wittenberg. Tickets for the series were sold for 75 cents.

It was in the fall of this same year that the Women's Guild of the church was, first organized. According to the record made by Henrietta Ayers in 1943, it was Mrs. Mason who brought the young women of the church together in November 1896. The first officers of the Guild were Mrs. John Whitman, president; Mrs. George Kelly, vice-president; Mrs. Charles Prickitt, secretary; and Mrs. Thorfin Tait, treasurer.[51] Probably the most spectacular event put on by the Guild in its early years was the darning fair in February 1897.[52] An advertisement ran in the local papers:

> Bachelors attention! The Presbyterian Church Improvement Guild invites all the bachelors to bring their undarned socks, gloves, or any articles needing repairs, to the lecture room on Monday evening, February 15 at eight o'clock, and they will be neatly and quickly mended by some of Metuchen's fairest damsels, and, while you wait, you will be refreshed by a cup of chocolate and a sandwich, to which your ten-cent admission ticket will entitle you.

Six booths were set up in the lecture room; one sold soap and washing boards, another flatirons and wax, another contained a sock mending table. The young ladies who did all the work were Nettie and Jennie Freeman, Jessie Mundy, Georgie Schenck, Lillie Van Sicklen, Etta Tappen, Caroline Carman, Elona Campbell, Zoe Edwards, Josie Flanagan, Grace Crowell and Irene Mason. The officers of the Guild helped to supervise the whole operation. The ladies evidently did an extensive business, for

158

the lecture room was crowded and a sum of money was raised to contribute to the building of the porch for the manse. The event drew much enthusiastic and favorable comment; it was said that the next day Metuchen's commuters looked spic and span in comparison with commuters from other towns.

During these years around the turn of the century, the church property was occasionally used for group meetings or events that were not directly connected with the activity of the church itself. In June of a numbers of years, the Board of Education of Raritan Township was granted the use of the church to hold closing exercises for the public schools.[53] In 1906 the church was used for a meeting of the New Jersey State Federation of Women's Clubs, and the same year a public meeting concerned with the victims of the San Francisco earthquake was held in the church.[54] In the spring of 1908 the Women's Christian Temperance Union was granted use of the Sunday School room for a cake sale.[55]

The great event of these years came in 1902 with the observance of the 25th anniversary of Mason's pastorate. Sunday, February 16, 1902, was the day for the official activities, with a major reception scheduled for the following day. The prayer service on Sunday morning at 10 was followed at 10:30 by the pastor's historical sermon. At 7:30 Sunday evening, a union service was held, with the pastors and choirs of St. Luke's Episcopal, Centenary Methodist, and Reformed Churches all taking part. In his historical sermon, the pastor recorded a rise in membership in his 25 years from 188 to 250 (figures recorded in Session minutes indicate membership at 200 in 1877 and 227 in 1902).[56] Mason performed 287 baptisms, officiated at 367 funerals and married 460 couples. Except for funerals for which there is no comparative information, all these figures are higher than for any previous 25 year period in the church's history. Mason's constant emphasis on benevolent giving had increased that figure from $158 in 1877 to $624 in 1902. The pastor cited a gift from Mrs. Ruth Thomas Watson which made possible the removal of the dilapidated fence around the church grounds, an innovation that Mason thought had begun a custom of open lawns which helped to beautify the town. Other legacies from John Watson, Erastus Freeman, and Benajah Mundy contributed importantly to the $70,000 spent on property improvements and current expenses over the 25 years. Besides those organizations already mentioned, Mason called attention to the formation of the Christian Endeavor Society and its Junior partner, and paid particular tribute to C. C. Campbell, who had been superintendent of the Sunday School for nearly 25 years, and, as it turned out, had many more to go. In concluding his sermon, Mason emphasized that the church should not live apart from the social, civic and business interest of the community. He had sought in his pastorate "to be in the midst of all human interests, to be a power for good, and to live for the community and not merely to live upon it."

The reception scheduled for the next day was postponed because of a heavy snow storm until Thursday, February 20.[57] Over 200 persons came to the lecture room that evening to honor the pastor. Charles Corbin, president of the Board of Trustees, presided and introduced a number of speakers. A. W. Marshall spoke for the Session, C. C. Campbell for the Sunday School, and Thomas M. Thickstun for the Young People's Christian Endeavor. Henry E. Ayers, treasurer, used his opportunity to remark that while he could easily take care of all coins received at Sunday services, he found it difficult to dispose of the buttons that were sometimes deposited in the collection plates. Mayor William Thornall and F. A. Pattison, president of the Village Library, added their congratulations. Messages were read from Honorable B. F. Howell, Congressman for the district, and from Henry M. Alden on behalf of Williams College. The clergy was represented by Rev. Joseph McNulty of the First Presbyterian Church of Woodbridge, Rev. George Payson of Rahway for the Presbytery of Elizabeth, and Rev. J. A. Liggett of Rahway who had given the charge to the pastor at his installation 25 years earlier. The pastor was presented with a

444

purse of $240 and the Improvement Guild gave him a silver salad spoon. The evening concluded with ice cream refreshments served by the Ladies Aid Society. Perhaps no one present realized that Rev. James Mason, then 60 years old, would come very close to doubling the length of his stay in the Metuchen Church, and would remain active in his community to the end of his life, still 36 years away.

CHAPTER XIV — FOOTNOTES

1. Biographical information from newspaper articles in Irene Mason Harper's collection, and in miscellaneous notes of William H. Ayers.
2. Mason tried to bring some of the immigrants working in the nearby claypits into the church, but he encountered objection from some of the established members. Information from interview with Irene Mason Harper, December 16, 1965.
3. Wallace N. Jamison, *Religion in New Jersey: A Brief History,* Princeton, 1964, 128-9.
4. Winthrop Hudson, *American Protestantism,* Chicago 1961, p. 78; Clifton E. Olmstead, *Religion in America, Past and Present,* Englewood Cliffs, New Jersey, 1961, 112-120.
5. Olmstead, *op cit.,* 117.
6. Winthrop Hudson, *The Great Tradition of the American Churches,* New York, 1963, chapter 8.
7. Olmstead, *op cit.,* 128-130.
8. Historical sermon delivered by Mason, February 16, 1902.
9. Sessional letter by Mason, January 1, 1879.
10. Session minutes, September 23, 1878; June 9, 1888.
11. David T. Marshall, *Recollections of Boyhood Days in Old Metuchen,* New York, 1929, p. 41.
12. *Ibid.,* 60.
13. This description is taken from an article in the Metuchen *Recorder* by Kay Rodney, and from notes of Irene Mason Harper.

14. Session minutes, September 11, 1877.
15. Sessional letter January 1, 1879. A gift from Ezra Hunt aided greatly.
16. Session minutes, September 29, 1885.
17. Session minutes, April 11, 1905.
18. Information taken from Secretary's Book of the Young Ladies Home Missionary Society, October 3, 1879 — June 1892.
19. Mason's historical sermon, February 16, 1902.
20. Information taken from minutes of meetings of Ladies Aid Society, 1888-1902.
21. Miscellaneous notes of William H. Ayers.
22. *Ibid.*
23. Mason's historical sermon, February 16, 1902.
24. J. Lloyd Grimstead manuscript on the First Presbyterian Church, 11-12; *Metuchen, The Brainy Borough,* unpublished, (hereafter referred to as Library Manuscript), ch. 2, 11-12; Session minutes, June 5, 1887. The land was sold for $1500.
25. Marshall, *Recollections, op. cit.,* 80-1.
26. Library manuscript, *op. cit.,* chapter on Fire Department, 2-3.
27. Session minutes 1881, 1886, *passim.*
28. Interview with Irene Mason Harper, December 16, 1965; Marshall, *Recollections, op. cit.,* 61-3. The exact date is uncertain, probably in 1877 or 1878. Edison's first demonstration of electric lights occurred outside his work laboratory in Menlo Park in December 1879, and in 1881 he built an electric railway from his laboratory to Dark Lane (Grove Avenue).
29. Library Manuscript, *op. cit.,* ch. 3, p. 4-5; miscellaneous notes loaned by the Edwin Risler family.
30. Library manuscript, *op. cit.,* ch. 9, p. 9; ch. 3, p. 5.
31. *Ibid.,* ch. 9, p. 8-9; Marshall, *Recollections, op. cit.,* 137-8.
32. Library manuscript, *op. cit.,* ch. 9, p. 5-6.
33. Superintendent C. C. Campbell's address, October 29, 1916 at the 100th Anniversary celebration of the Sabbath School.
34. Session minutes, May 31, 1890.
35. Interview with Irene Mason Harper, December 16, 1965.

36. The printed sermon is in the scrapbook loaned by Mrs. Harper.
37. This account of the General Assembly meeting was taken from numerous press articles from Detroit newspapers, as well as New Brunswick and Metuchen papers, collected in Mrs. Harper's scrapbook.
38. Mrs. Harper's scrapbook contains a mass of material, mostly in defense of Briggs.
39. New Brunswick *Daily Fredonian,* May 19, 1891.
40. Jamison, *Religion in New Jersey, op. cit.,* 130.
41. Interview with Irene Mason Harper, December 16, 1965.
42. This account taken from Mrs. Harper's scrapbook.
43. New Brunswick *Home News,* March 29, April 4, 1904.
44. Mrs. Harper's scrapbook; Library manuscript, ch. 3, p. 1; ch. 2, p. 14-15.
45. Session minutes February 21,25, 28, March 3, 1894.
46. Mason's historical sermon, February 16, 1902.
47. *Ibid.*
48. *Ibid.;* Session minutes, March 4, 1899.
49. Session minutes, July 1, 1895.
50. Information about these talks was taken from the poster.
51. Record made by Henrietta Ayers, February 25, 1943.
52. This account taken from the New York *Herald Tribune,* February 15, 1897; several articles are in the scrapbook loaned by Mrs. Harper.
53. Session minutes, May 12, 1901, as one example.
54. Session minutes, April 22, 1906.
55. Session minutes, February 23 and May 10, 1908.
56. The historical sermon is printed in newspaper articles in Mrs. Harper's scrapbook.
57. This account taken from newspaper articles in Mrs. Harper's scrapbook and from Session minutes, September 7, 1902.

Chapter XV

MASON: HIS TWENTIETH CENTURY CAREER

"The Session records with gratitude that on May 21, 1918 the Borough of Metuchen voted to banish all liquor saloons from the Borough by 32 majority."
— Session minutes, May 29, 1918

"For Congress — vote for Dr. James Gilbert Mason, Independent Fusion Dry. The only candidate openly for the whole Constitution and the Coolidge enforcement policy.
"I believe the heart of our country is dry and when the conscientious Christian voters unite in the effort to elect dry representatives and place in control of enforcement a party entirely dry, the liquor traffic will be entirely abolished ..."
*— Political card on Mason's candidacy for Congress
in 1926, and his own statement thereon.*

THE YEARS UP TO the World War saw continued efforts to keep the church buildings in good condition. In 1907 the Guild helped to raise money to lay linoleum in the vestibule of the church, and new carpeting on the stairs leading to the galleries.[1] In 1908 an asbestos slate roof replaced the shingle roof, and a contract for a new organ was let. To meet

165

the $2500 expense for the organ, the pastor was able to secure a $1000 donation from Andrew Carnegie, and the rest of the money was obtained from various balances without disturbing the invested real estate trust fund.[2] Another major improvement was undertaken in 1912 with new hardwood flooring and new carpet for the pulpit, steps and aisles of the church at a cost of over $1200.[3]

The Guild conducted a wide variety of social events in order to raise funds. There were food sales, sales at Christmas and Easter, musicals and recitals, a paper social, a dime social, a rubber social, a thimble bee, and numerous luncheons and suppers. The rubber social was held in 1909 pursuant to a report that if the Guild could collect at least 2000 pounds of old rubber in any form, it could be sold to a Philadelphia dealer for four cents a pound.[4] In 1915-16 the Guild raised $100 to have an electric blower installed in the church organ. A collection to benefit this fund was taken at an exhibit of Edison's old and new phonographs in April 1915, arranged by Dr. Mason.[5]

In addition to these activities, the Guild helped to supervise the music program of the church. During the World War the group working on surgical dressings completed over 8000 articles, and the committee working for Belgium Relief completed 61 garments. Small donations were made to the Recreation House Fund at Camp Dix.[6]

For its part, the Ladies Aid Society paid the organist's salary, gave dinners and enjoyed their social occasions at the shore or elsewhere. Of some interest may be two menus discussed for their dinners. One included clam chowder, roast beef, pork, corned beef, baked beans, potato salad, salmon salad, sweet potatoes, apple and cranberry sauce, cakes, coffee and tea.[7] Another included soup, fresh ham, spring lamb, peas, potatoes, jellies, pickles, raised biscuits, ice cream, cake and coffee.[8] Mrs. Phebe Martin served for 30 years as president of the society, from 1896 until the day of her death on November 29, 1926.

The Aid Society conducted a good-natured social rivalry with the Men's Brotherhood. This organization was formed in 1908 in an effort, conducted throughout the denomination by the General Assembly, to interest men in the activities of Christian fellowship and works of Christian usefulness; William T. Campbell was the first president. The Brotherhood held both religious and social meetings for men, involved men in missionary and benevolent operations, welcomed strangers who came to church, and visited the sick and prospective new members. The fragments of minutes for the year 1915 when William H. Ayers was president showed discussions about the need for more Sunday School teachers, more church ushers, arranging a Sunday School excursion to Ocean Grove, and playing a ball game with a club from the Reformed Church.[9] Probably the most successful event carried out by the Brotherhood in these years was a minstrel show in December 1914, with many songs and dances, and numerous jokes directed at prominent church members and townsmen. A large audience of 350 attended, and the $100 that was raised was contributed to the construction of sidewalk along the west side of Main Street.[10]

The Session in these years became involved in an increasing variety of tasks, though its personnel changed only very slowly because of almost automatic reelection. In 1907 Mason notified Session that he had recovered old Session records "dating back to 1717, date of the first meeting house."[11] A communication opposing licensing of another saloon in Metuchen was adopted, endorsed by the pastor and clerk, and forwarded to Judge Booream of the County Court.[12] On other occasions, Session was concerned with the purchase of communion glasses, consideration of grading Sunday School classes, granting use of the church for various meetings, and organizing union services in Holy Week and at Thanksgiving.[13] In 1911 an Interchurch Federation of Metuchen was formed, a council to be composed of the minister and one elected layman from the Reformed, Baptist, Methodist, Episcopal and Presbyterian churches.[14]

The envelope system was adopted for benevolent giving in 1909, with about one-third of benevolences going to foreign missions, one-third to home missions, and one-third to a variety of causes in education, capital expense, ministerial relief, temperance, and so forth. The change appeared to have positive results as far as improved benevolent giving was concerned.[15] Further efforts to improve giving by the congregation were made in March 1917 with Session's decision to adopt the "Every Member program" as recommended by the General Assembly. A committee was formed and volunteers were sought to canvass the members. The appeal was to be based on a budget submitted to the congregation in April for their approval, and this was to be followed by letters to members stating the financial needs and accompanied by pledge cards.[16] The canvass committee subsequently reported that visits were made to 110 families on one Sunday afternoon and that the financial results were "more immediately productive than some of us had imagined possible."[17] For church operations, twenty-five new pledges and ten increased ones were received, and for benevolence, ten new and seven increased.

Two events of major importance in the church occurred in these years. One was the commissioning of Irene Mason, the pastor's daughter, as missionary to India and her marriage to Rev. Arthur E. Harper in November 1914. The commissioning of the two missionaries occurred at a service on November 15, with Dr. Mason presiding, an address by Harry Hicks, general secretary of the missionary education movement, and the charge to the new missionaries given by Rev. William Schell of the Presbyterian Board of Foreign Missions.[18] Two days later Dr. Mason, assisted by the pastor of the Central Church in Newark, married his daughter to the Rev. Harper. Within a few days the two sailed for Lahore, India to begin together their missionary career.

The other event was the centennial celebration of the Sabbath School in the fall of 1916. Friday evening October 27, Superintendent C. C. Campbell gave an historical address looking back to the founding of the school in 1816 when, under Superintendent William Ross, it was first held in the old Franklin School.[19] On its 100th birthday almost 200 students and teachers took part in the active program held in the academy building. The festive days of the year were Harvest Home, Christmas, Easter, Children's Day and Rally Day, and there was always an annual picnic in June. An active Men's Bible class numbered 40, and there was also an adult class for women. A special religious service was held on Sunday afternoon October 29 to commemorate the anniversary.

The World War touched the church relatively lightly. Twenty-two members served in the armed forces; one, Edward O. Fugel, gave his life.[20] During the war, a joint committee was formed from several of the borough's churches to provide hospitality for the troops stationed at Camp Raritan in Bonhamtown. The Campbell house, on Amboy near Main, was rented and operated as a social center for soldiers on leave.[21]

During the second decade of the twentieth century Mason carried his crusade against alcohol into the public arena of politics. He was already a well known figure as a clergyman and as a leader of the temperance movement. In politics he had generally favored the Republican party, but Progressivism did not appeal to him and the Bull Moose campaign of Theodore Roosevelt disillusioned him. He soon became a Prohibitionist, convinced that the advocates of temperance were also the best of progressives, because they favored women's rights and the principle of referendum and recall. After an unsuccessful effort to become a state senator in 1912, he was chosen by the National Prohibition Party in 1913, at the age of 72, to be its candidate for governor of New Jersey. His acceptance speech, delivered in the high school auditorium on June 16, called for the destruction of the liquor power which had been entrenched in the national government since the Civil War. To Mason the liquor traffic was the basic cause of everything he regarded as a social evil, including lawlessness, corrupt political machines, high taxes and mounting debt. "Pick up the thread of any evil, follow it, and you will reach the saloon."[22] Mason carried on an extensive campaign in the summer and fall of 1913, and though he was not elected, it was estimated that his campaign had helped to defeat the Republican candidate by splitting the Republican vote and thereby electing the Democrat James Fielder to the office.[23]

The vigor and enthusiasm displayed by Mason in the campaign soon led to efforts to get him to run for higher office. A banquet and rally of Middlesex County Prohibitionists held at the Presbyterian Church launched a boom for Mason as the party's national candidate for President of the United States. At the State Prohibition Convention in Trenton in May 1916 the Middlesex delegation strongly endorsed Mason's candidacy, and state and county leaders rapidly fell into line. Mason was temporary chairman of this state convention and in his keynote address, he continued to relate as many bad things as possible to the evils of liquor. "The women of New Jersey in their fight to obtain the right to vote were defeated, to the lasting shame of the state, by the rum power in the state."

At the national convention of the Prohibition Party at St. Paul, Minnesota in July 1916, Mason's name was presented to the convention as New Jersey's first choice for the nomination. At the age of 75, the high point of this Presbyterian minister's political career came on the first ballot. Mason was fourth among a dozen candidates, and the nomination went to Frank Hanly of Indiana, to whom Mason pledged his full support.

All of this effort at the national level did not lead to disinterest in what was happening closer to home. In 1917 and 1918 Mason led the fight in Metuchen to outlaw saloons altogether, and in the local option election of May 21, 1918, the drys won, 278-246; four licensed saloons eventually had to close. On May 29, the Session of the church "records with gratitude that on May 21, 1918, the Borough of Metuchen voted to banish all liquor saloons from the Borough by 32 majority; also that by order of the Federal Government the five mile limit law was enforced around Camp Raritan, abolishing nineteen saloons in adjoining townships."[24] Mason also helped to develop evidence leading to the appointment of a receiver for a wholesale liquor business at Ford's Corner.[25]

After the passage of the 18th Amendment and the Volstead Act, Mason campaigned against bootlegging and in favor of law enforcement, an activity he seemed to enjoy whether it was at local, state or national level. In 1923 he applauded Governor George Silzer's analysis of many state problems in the governor's inaugural address. "But when he came to treat of prohibition it was revealed that his intellectual machinery had stopped twenty years ago.... His talk on temperance sounds much like an excerpt out of the year book of the United States Brewers Association.... Patriotic people ... must not go to sleep while the brewers and politicians are plotting against the moral welfare."[26] Anyone who attacked the 18th Amendment was really attacking all law enforcement.

> There is a noisy minority filled with the lowest form of greed, and appealing to a degenerate appetite financed by beer and bootleg money, which is crying 'the law cannot be enforced ...' The attack is upon all law and if successful must lead to a chaotic and lawless world, wherein life, personal liberty, property rights, human happiness and all human welfare are in danger....[27]

In 1926 Mason, now 85 years old, and recently retired from the pulpit, decided to launch an independent political career. He wrote a letter to the *Recorder* complaining that Harold Hoffman, mayor of South Amboy and candidate for Congress, had not taken a stand on the 18th Amendment and the Volstead Act. A week later, referring to the Presbyterian General Assembly statement that the 18th Amendment was "the greatest moral reform of this generation," Mason declared himself a candidate for Congress on an Independent Fusion Dry platform.[28] He distributed flyers in which he claimed to be "the only candidate openly for the whole Constitution and the Coolidge enforcement policy." On the back of one of these flyers, he wrote, "I believe the heart of our country is dry and when the conscientious Christian voters unite in the effort to elect dry representatives and place in control of enforcement a party entirely dry, the liquor traffic will be entirely abolished ..." Defeated again, he had yet one more effort to make when he ran as the Prohibition party's candidate for United States Senator in 1930 to fill the unexpired term of Senator Walter Edge. Here he opposed repeal because he thought it would lead to a revival of states rights doctrines. He ridiculed a Literary Digest poil showing preference for repeal by saying it was "a scheme to gain subscriptions and centered on the wet spots of the country."[29] Republican Dwight Morrow was the victorious candidate.

None of the defeats Mason suffered convinced him that he was wrong in his espousal of prohibition and law enforcement as the saviors of society. In an interview he gave to the New Brunswick *Sunday Times* in 1934, he saw no future for either major political party. "Both should be dumped into the waste basket of history!"[30] The Prohibition party was "the only one qualified to ... save us from the threatened national immorality, moral decay, destruction of family life by divorce, decay of social ideals, and all sorts of crimes, so greatly increased since the repeal of the 18th Amendment." When asked by the interviewer who he considered the most remarkable people he knew, he named Mark Hopkins, famed teacher and president of Williams College when Mason was a student there, and Frances Willard, temperance crusader, leader of the W.C.T.U., and one of the founders of the Prohibition party.

During the years after the first World War Protestantism was losing much of its vitality and creativeness. Presbyterians, particularly, were deeply divided over the controversy between modernists and fundamentalists.[31] In New Jersey, Catholic churches were growing faster than those of any Protestant denomination.[32] The enthusiasm and dedication of the pre-war years were absent, church attendance declined, Sunday School and Bible classes suffered from lack of interest.[33] Church groups placed more emphasis on purely social gatherings without the dedication to the purposes of Christian fellowship. Protestantism was losing its dynamic force and becoming, like the society as a whole, more secular.[34] Inevitably these changes were reflected in the last years of Mason's pastorate, even though he tried with all his native vigor to stem the tide that he saw engulfing the church.

As if to mark a new era, two of the long time leaders of the church died in the early months of 1920. A resolution by Session on February 15 marked the death of R. Bruce Crowell, 42 years an elder, 33 years clerk of the Session, a man who had likewise served his community through a long career on the Board of Education. Another resolution on April 11 noted the death of C. C. Campbell, 54 years a trustee, 30 years superintendent of the Sunday School, and 27 years as deacon and elder.[35] Church membership in these years climbed slowly from 253 in 1920 to 300 in 1924, the last full year of Mason's pastorate. A brief effort to conduct a revival in the church occurred in January 1922 when an evangelist from Tennessee came to lead a series of meetings. Though apparently attended by a large number of people, the revival produced only a small financial return, and did not lead to any substantial increase in church membership.[36] In May of that same year the Session approved the establishment of a Daily Vacation Bible School, to run for five weeks in the lecture room beginning July 10.[37]

In these years the Women's Guild actively worked to raise money for a variety of purposes. The most successful undertaking financially was the annual bazaar in the fall. In 1921, for instance, the bazaar raised over $450. Six tables were organized: fancy, candy, apron, doll, food and cake. In addition pop corn and punch were served, some paintings were for sale, there was a post office window, and a cafeteria. The Guild contributed funds for interior decoration of the church in 1922 and in 1925 undertook the major task of paying for the recushioning and recurtaining of the church at a total cost of $1,314.50.[38] On the other hand the ladies decided not to install a pay telephone in the lecture room because of the excessive cost.[39] In 1922 the Guild spent time cutting unbleached muslin into garments destined for Near East Relief Work.[40] The chief social events of these years were auto ride picnics. The home of Mrs. John Reynolds in Montclair was one favorite destination. In the fall of 1923, "Five cars left the Pharmacy about ten o'clock, with a company of twenty-three women and one baby boy. The weather was perfect, and everyone was in the best of spirits. The drive to Montclair was taken by way of the Reservation; it was worthwhile following the winding paths through the beautiful woods."[41]

The Men's Brotherhood, sponsor of the Men's Bible Class, was also very active in these years. The annual banquet in 1924 brought 175 men to a dinner served by their friendly rivals, the Ladies Aid Society. Speakers at the affair were A. Harry Moore, Commissioner of Parks and Public Property in Jersey City, and Rev. Cordie J. Culp, pastor of the Presbyterian Church in New Brunswick.[42] The evening's entertainment was carried on in a light-hearted mood. There were songs, for which Miss Zoe Edwards, the Brotherhood's only woman member, played the piano. The printed program was filled with humorous remarks about church members. For instance:

> When poverty comes in at the door, love flies out the window, is an old proverb. In this community it has been changed to read: When the 7:21 pulls in at the depot, Ed flies out the door.[43]
>
> Charlie's favorite hymn when he sees a flapper - Look Ye Saints the Sight is Glorious.[44]

The serious message occupied its place as well, from one of the officers, or the pastor. The program for the 1926 banquet included a letter from Dr. Mason, then in Jacksonville, Florida, that he regretted not being able to come to the annual dinner. The message of the pastor, Rev. George Humphries, stressed the need for attendance at church service, and the officers emphasized the value of religious education for men through such groups as the Men's Bible class.[45]

By 1923 the end of Mason's long pastorate was drawing near. In March of that year, Anita, whom he had married in the church nearly 42 years before, died, an event that saddened him very greatly.[46] His health declined somewhat, and in the fall of 1924 the Session offered to grant Mason a leave of absence to recover his health, but he refused. Rev. George Humphries presided at Session meetings in November and on November 30 the Session acted to give Mason five months leave of absence with full salary beginning January 1, 1925. A pulpit supply committee was set up to provide for services; Rev. Humphries occupied the pulpit during much of this time.[47] A joint meeting of elders, deacons and trustees, held in the early spring, adopted an important resolution. Noting the "uncertain degree of health" and the "advanced age" of the pastor, the resolution stated,

> ... it is therefore with the greatest reluctance, and with the most tender and anxious thought for his welfare that nevertheless we feel constrained to take positive constructive action ... it is the sense of the meeting that the Pastorate of Dr. Mason be terminated at the expiration of his leave of absence, and that our church obligate itself to pay him a retirement pension of at least $50 per month for the remainder of his life....[48]

A letter containing the resolution was forwarded to Mason in Orlando, Florida. He replied requesting a further extension of his leave, and a raise in his pension to $65. A second joint meeting of elders, deacons and trustees on April 10 rejected Mason's request for an extension of leave because of the need for the church to be functioning better than it was. Daily pastoral work was badly needed; collections were declining; the church could not afford a higher pension. The manse was to be surrendered on June 1. Mason's second reply, on May 6, accepted these conditions. He asked the Session to join in his request to Presbytery that the pastoral relation be dissolved and that he be relieved of his pastoral duties effective June 1.[49] A congregational meeting on June 1 accepted these decisions and Presbytery was notified. A special resolutions committee, representing the various organizations in the church, was appointed to present a suitable resolution on Dr. Mason's ministry. The resolution, adopted by the congregation on June 14, read as follows:

> Resolved, that the congregation, Societies and Officers of First Presbyterian Church of Metuchen ... desire to signify their appreciation of the long and faithful pastorate of Dr. Mason extending even to the third and fourth generation of many families in the parish; and further be it resolved, that we regret the necessity which brings this service to a close and desire to record this token of appreciation and a hope that he may be returned to health and strength to enjoy the rest and pleasure so richly deserved.[50]

Dr. Mason returned to Metuchen to preach at the regular service on June 21, and then declared the pulpit vacant.[51] On September 23, 1925, a congregational meeting elected George Humphries pastor at a salary of $2,600, free use of the manse, and a month's annual vacation.[52] The long ministry had finally come to an end.

An era had ended, but not a life. Having been freed of the daily burden of a practicing ministry, this 83-year-old man attacked with renewed vigor some of his favorite targets, and undertook journeys that would have stopped men much younger than he. After the failure of his congressional campaign in 1926, he undertook the long and difficult journey to India to visit his daughter Irene. Later, in 1934, he attended the centennial celebration of Delta Upsilon fraternity at Williams College. At 93 years of age, he was its oldest living member. He wrote to Irene that he had given a talk at the fraternity's banquet, and he was proud that he was the only one whose voice could be heard by everyone present.[53] Probably one of his last short trips occurred in 1937 when he went to Menlo Park to participate in the laying of the cornerstone of the Edison Tower.[54]

Mason continued to make his voice heard to defend the sanctity of the Sabbath. In 1932 he requested the Metuchen police to put a stop to football playing on Sunday.[55] Apparently the request caused considerable comment; the police refused to act, however, because they would have had to undertake the impossible task of enforcing all other blue laws as well. In a letter to William H. Ayers written from Atlantic City on October 30, 1934, Mason commented on a newspaper report that a Sunday ball game between Metuchen and Freehold had prominently mentioned the participation of Humphries, son of the church's pastor. He wrote, "I wonder can a man be in good and regular standing in the Presbyterian Church and be a leader of Sunday Ball Games?"[56]

Mason's 95th birthday in October, 1936, brought a personal note of congratulations from Herbert K. England, stated clerk of the Presbytery of Elizabeth. On Christmas Day that year he wrote to Irene, in a handwriting still large and bold, "I am full of Christmas cards and New Year's gaiety ... I am thankful for all these lengthening years, full of God's blessings ... I daily send up thanksgivings for all his benefits... my heart overflows with gratitude."[57]

On Friday evening, March 18, 1938, Mason's life came to a quiet end in his home at 32 William Street. His death was widely reported in metropolitan newspapers; the funeral service in the church on Monday the 21st was conducted by Rev. Roland Bahnson of Plainfield, moderator of Elizabeth Presbytery. Rev. Cordie Gulp of New Brunswick gave a funeral address, and pastors of Presbyterian churches in Rahway, Basking Ridge and Cranford also took part. Mason's son, Gilbert, wrote a long letter to Irene on March 22 that their father had passed away peacefully without pain; the funeral service was beautiful and dignified, and Gulp impressive in expression and voice. The whole front of the church was banked high with flowers. Burial took place in the church cemetery.

Over a year later on May 14, 1939, a bronze tablet commemorating Mason's influence on the moral, spiritual and intellectual life of Metuchen and the church was dedicated at a special service, and placed on the wall at the rear of the church. More than 62 years before, James Mason had first preached from its pulpit.

CHAPTER XV — FOOTNOTES

1. Guild record of Henrietta Ayers, February 25, 1943; minutes of Women's Guild, September 10, 1907.
2. Insertion in Session minutes of report made by Trustees to Session on year 1907-8.
3. Annual report of Guild, February 6, 1913.
4. Guild minutes, September 27 and October 11, 1909.
5. *Ibid.*, February 5, March 9, 1915; March 14, 1916.
6. *Ibid.*, November 1917, September 24, 1918; February 11, 1919.
7. Ladies Aid Society, minutes, October 6, 1909.
8. *Ibid.*, April 3, 1912.
9. Minutes of Brotherhood, 1915.
10. Metuchen *Recorder*, December 19, 1914.
11. Session minutes, April 14, 1907. It is of interest that the second phrase in this quotation was in a different handwriting than the first, and that the last 7 in 1717 was written over a 5.
12. Session minutes, April 12, 1908.
13. Session minutes, December 27, 1908; November 12, 1911.
14. Session minutes, December 9, 1911.
15. Session minutes, February 28, 1909; February 5, 1911.
16. Session minutes, March 7, April 1 and 7, 1917.
17. Session minutes, May 9, 1917.
18. A report of the service is in the Session book.
19. Metuchen *Recorder*, November 9, 1916; also typewritten copy of Campbell's address.
20. William H. Ayers, *A History of the Presbyterian Church,* Metuchen, 1947, p. 30; *Metuchen, The Brainy Borough,* unpublished, (hereinafter referred to as Library Manuscript), ch. 4, p. 3-4.

178

21. Library manuscript, ch. 4, p. 3-4.
22. This account of some of the highlights of Mason's political career is written from numerous newspaper articles in the scrapbook loaned by Mrs. Harper.
23. New Brunswick *Daily Home News*, January 18, 1924. The Republican's total of about 140,000 was the smallest vote for a Republican gubernatorial candidate since 1892.
24. Session minutes, May 29, 1918.
25. New Brunswick *Daily Home News*, May 14, 1919.
26. Letter by Mason in New Brunswick *Daily Home News*, January 20, 1923.
27. New Brunswick *Daily Home News*, January 18, 1924.
28. Metuchen *Recorder,* May 19 and 26, 1926.
29. Newark *Evening Press,* May 17, 1930.
30. New Brunswick *Sunday Times,* August 12, 1934.
31. Wallace N. Jamison, *Religion in New Jersey: A Brief History,* Princeton 1964, 150-1.
32. *Ibid.,* 161.
33. Winthrop Hudson, *The Great Tradition of the American Churches,* New York 1963, chapter 9.
34. *Ibid.,* 198.
35. Session minutes, February 15, April 11, 1920.
36. Session minutes, May 12, 22, August 3, November 9, 1921; January 19, 1922.
37. Session minutes, May 5, 1922.
38. Guild minutes, September and December, 1922; May 13, 1925; Annual Report, February 1926.
39. Guild minutes, December 12, 1923; January 9, 1924.
40. Guild minutes, June 1, 1922.
41. Guild minutes, October 10, 1923.
42. Session minutes, May 7, 1924.
43. Program of 16th Annual Banquet, May 6, 1924.
44. Program of 18th Annual Banquet, March 19, 1926.
45. *Ibid.*
46. Session minutes, March 4, 1923. The Session relieved him from preaching duties for the month of March.

47. Session minutes, November 9, 12, 30, December 3, 1924.
48. This meeting was probably held March 17, 1925, though the Session record says April. The letter to Mason containing the resolution was dated March 19, and the next meeting to consider Mason's reply was on April 10.
49. Session minutes, May 12, 1925.
50. Session minutes, June 14, 1925.
51. Session minutes, June 21, 1925.
52. Session minutes, September 23, 1925.
53. Newspaper articles and letters in Mrs. Harper's scrapbook.
54. New York *Herald Tribune,* July 2, 1937.
55. Metuchen *Recorder,* October 7, 1932.
56. In miscellaneous notes of William H. Ayers.
57. Mrs. Harper's scrapbook.

Chapter XVI

GEORGE HUMPHRIES — THE CHURCH
IN THE DEPRESSION

"... he had to preach the Word, in season and out, to a people caught in the icy grip of a national depression.... Through the weekly sessions of the Bible Class ... he applied the Gospel to man's social condition as reflected in the economic and social dislocations of human lives.... He restored hope to men disillusioned by job losses, driven to despair by their inability to provide for their families...."
           – Letter of Rev. Bertram Humphries, Feb. 1, 1967

THE ECONOMIC DEPRESSION of the 1930s had a deep social impact upon both the church and the community. The need to minister to men who were unable to find jobs and to provide for their families proved to be a difficult experience, especially for Presbyterians whose economic status was more likely to be secure and substantial. It was fortunate that the church's minister, Rev. George Humphries, understood this need better than many of his congregation, and was able to contribute both spiritually and practically to the solution of these serious problems. George Humphries came naturally to the Christian ministry, both his father and his brother having served long pastorates in New England Methodist

181

churches.[1] He studied at Brown University and graduated from Andover-Newton Theological Seminary. He preached in Presbyterian churches in Troy, New York and Tamaqua, Pennsylvania before coming to Metuchen to succeed Mason. Humphries had always been attracted to working with people in secular as well as spiritual matters. During World War I he served as personnel manager at the Alabama Dry Dock and Shipbuilding Company in Mobile, and he later occupied a similar position with Esso's Bayway Refinery in Elizabeth. At the age of 48 he was called to the pastorate in Metuchen and was officially installed on October 7, 1925. His father, Rev. Elijah Humphries, gave the charge to the pastor, and his predecessor, Rev. James Mason, gave the charge to the congregation.[2]

In his first year, Humphries reorganized the work and activities of the church into eight major divisions, with an elder in charge of each. These were advertising, to publish the monthly church bulletin; visitation, organized by districts; prayer meeting; Sunday School; Christian Endeavor; evening service, conducted by the Brotherhood or by one of the women's groups; Brotherhood, to supply ushers; and music, with immediate plans to establish a new Junior Choir.[3] Subsequently, general planning conferences were held, with representatives of all the various organizations of the church present.[4] Under the spur of these efforts, membership in the church gradually rose, reaching a peak of 415 in 1929. Quarterly communions were observed on the first Sundays of January, April, July and October; each quarter there was also a special Sunday on behalf of benevolence.[5] For a while an experiment was made to start the church service at 11:15 in order to allow sufficient time for Sunday School to be dismissed. The church bell rang first at 9:30, then from 9:58-10 to signal the start of Sunday School, 10:58-11 to end Sunday School and 11:13-11:15 to mark the beginning of church service.[6] The problem of getting the church service started promptly, however, apparently remained unsolved. Session later decided that the real solution lay in better cooperation between the organist, the sexton and the choir leader.[7]

Sunday School enrollment reached 250 in these years and the problem of accommodations became acute. The situation had been discussed in 1929, and plans were drawn in 1930 for a new, two-story brick educational building to be erected west of the church. The structure was completed in 1931 and dedicated on June 14 when the keys to the building were turned over to Paul Prather, superintendent of the Sunday School.[8] Better facilities, improved organization and increased membership brought an expansion of Session to ten elders, and at the congregation meeting to take this action, it was announced that either men or women were eligible for election.[9] The congregation, however, refused to break the traditional pattern and the first women elders were not elected until 1966. In order better to supervise the spiritual guidance of the people, elders and deacons were placed in charge of assigned lists of parishioners.[10]

Humphries had a distinct interest in the history of the Metuchen church. In 1931 he appointed two elders to meet with him as a committee to collect relevant documents and records. During the fall of that year, Mrs. Ralph Seiler collected some letters and documents which were placed in the church vault; later, efforts were made to enlist the aid of Rev. James Mason.[11] In 1935 additional records were deposited, including material on the centennial celebration of the Sunday School in 1916, and the historical address delivered by William H. Ayers in 1934. During the latter year the church made plans to observe the 140th anniversary of the first resident pastor, Henry Cook. The celebration began with a communion service on Sunday, December 2. On Wednesday evening, December 5, a general congregation meeting was held, at which Rev. Earle Devanny of the Woodbridge Presbyterian Church addressed the gathering; an exhibit of colonial church literature was displayed in the Educational Building. On Sunday evening, December 9, Elder William H. Ayers gave an address on the history of the church and presented to the church a silhouette of Henry Cook.[12] Congratulatory messages on the anniversary were received from Rev. Fred Druckenmiller, moderator of Elizabeth Presbytery, from Governor A. Harry Moore, and from Harold Hoffman, Commissioner of Motor Vehicles. A few years later, in 1939, the tablet in memory of Rev. James Mason was unveiled in the church. Finally, in 1941 the pastor organized a membership drive to bring in 175 new members as a goal to be reached by what he considered to be the 175th Anniversary of the church in 1942.[13] Though Session considered holding such a celebration, none ever took place.[14] The pastor apparently believed that the evidence for the church's founding in 1717 was too slim to be reliable, and that 1767 was a more accurate date.

By far the most serious problem of Humphries' tenure, and by all odds the thing that made his pastorate noteworthy was his Christian and human effort to cope with the impact of the depression, not only on his own congregation, but especially upon the community itself. Probably the greatest contribution that Humphries made to make life more meaningful and more bearable in adversity was the weekly Men's Bible Class which he organized and conducted. Its membership was interdenominational and community-wide; its average attendance was about 100, with a peak enrollment of 300, and the class was successfully conducted for ten years.[15] Humphries tried to apply the teaching of the Gospel to the problems of severe economic and social dislocation in individual lives, and tried to replace despair with hope, disillusionment with comfort and strength. Surely this was an outstanding example of Christian outreach at a time of great need; yet some members of Session were critical of this and other community activities of the pastor, and thought he should spend more time in his professional duties in the church.[16]

At the height of the depression, Humphries served for several years without pay as the first Director of Public Welfare for the Borough of Metuchen. In 1932 some 900 residents of the town were on relief and in subsequent years of that decade the usual number was about 200.[17] Annual appropriations for relief were a major part of the municipal budget. Humphries distributed coal, food, and supplies to the poor and needy as fairly as he could; his experience and reputation brought him an appointment to the County Welfare Commission, a position he held even after his retirement from the pulpit.[18]

Humphries' son, Bertram, characterized his father as a "down-to-earth preacher of the Gospel," whose sermons constantly tried to show the relevance of Biblical texts for the practical problems that people had to face. The emphasis of his day was less on theology, creed and Cross, and more on individual morality and the Golden Rule; less on organization and administration and more on the essential mission of helpfulness and guidance for the individual.[19] Inevitably the congregation included families that were poor and adversely affected by the depression, though that became less true by the late years of Humphries' pastorate. Compromises and economies had to be made in the church budgets. Humphries' salary was cut from $3000 to $2700, and needed repair and maintenance to the manse was postponed until 1942 and later.[20] Though membership reached its peak in this pastorate with 459 in 1934, the total financial contribution from the congregation did not again reach the 1929 level of about $11,200 except for the year 1931. After 1934 membership dropped off gradually to 340 in 1941, the last full year of Humphries' pastorate.[21]

Yet the organizations of the church were very active in these years. The Women's Guild emphasized social affairs, luncheons (usually at Pfaff's restaurant), and entertainments, using proceeds from a large number of functions for various needs of the church. In the spring of 1934, for instance, the Guild held a St. Patrick's Day social and hat trimming party; a fashion parade of the '80s ("... many an attic was raided for that program...."); and the annual outing at Mrs. Witmer's home in Lavallette.[22] The next year's programs included a Children's Easter Circus in April, a picnic at Roosevelt Park, and a food demonstration on salads and sandwiches by a home economist from Public Service; in 1936 a minstrel show was the season's highlight.[23] Attendance and interest were very high, and the annual bazaar in November usually brought in over $200. Funds were spent toward reupholstering pulpit furniture, replacing choir curtains, and recovering leather doors at the rear of the church; profits of the bazaar were contributed to the Decoration Fund.[24] In addition, donations were frequently made to Kiddie Keep Well Camp and to the County Tuberculosis League.[25] Earlier, in 1930, the Guild had contributed $500 toward the new Educational Building.[26]

The Women's Missionary Society was likewise very active in these years, sponsoring talks on various countries of the world, usually in Africa and the Orient, where missionaries were active, and contributing money, clothing and hospital supplies to both national and foreign missions. The Society's major social event was the annual Irene Harper tea in October. In 1940 Rev. and Mrs. Harper were present at the occasion, on furlough from their mission in the Punjab in India.[27] In 1941 Mrs. Harper was honored at the tea with a life membership in the National Board of Foreign Missions Society. She spoke to the group of conditions in India, emphasizing that the people there were much less concerned with the care of their own aged and helpless members than they were about the cows that were present everywhere.[28] The Society's financial report for 1936-7 showed $290 credited to foreign mission work, and $200 to national missions. Through the Presbytery of Elizabeth, missionary work was supported in Arizona, North Carolina, Tennessee, Utah, Alaska, Cuba, Puerto Rico, Mexico; also India, Siam, Formosa, Japan and Persia.[29] In 1937 and 1938 Mrs. Humphries served as president of the Society.

Presbytery met at Metuchen February 1, 1940, to ordain Bertram E. Humphries, the pastor's son, to the ministry. Bertram had been united with the Metuchen Church in Mason's last year. He subsequently graduated from Metuchen High School, and from Brown University, and in 1939 received a Bachelor of Divinity degree from Union Theological Seminary.[30] The ordination sermon was delivered by Rev. Henry Sloane Coffin, president of Union Seminary, the prayer of ordination given by

Rev. Chester Davis, vice-moderator of Presbytery, and the charge to the candidate by his father. Subsequently, Rev. Humphries was assigned to the Presbytery of Syracuse, N. Y.

The late years of Humphries' tenure were marked by the first hints of social changes brought by the war and its effects that were to become rapidly more important and within a few years were to work a major transformation in the church and in its relation to its community. The unsettling influence of the war crisis on society and on church membership became a matter of widespread concern among the officers of the church within a few months of the outbreak of the Second World War. In the fall of 1940, elders and trustees in joint meeting expressed concern that the church should develop a more active program of social events to create more interest among the members and to increase financial contributions. The Session was urged to allow use of the social room for card parties as a means of raising revenue.[31] In addition, a letter from Cora Edwards to Session advocated formation of a Council of Religious Education to stimulate Christian educational programs among both young people and adults, and to counteract what seemed to be a loss of spirituality.

> "In these terrible days boys and girls, men and women are dropping out of this church because they do not find what they want.... About a dozen young men have dropped out in the last year or two — the future support of the church — and we do nothing except possibly to blame the pastor or the Sunday School superintendent.... I have never seen spiritual religion at so low an ebb as at present."[32]

In 1941 a Board of Religious Education was established and began to work through committees.[33] But the real answer to the need for greater attention to social activity was not to come until the development of plans for the social center a few years later.

187

Another portent of the future was a report to Session from Presbytery in 1941 that there was an increasing need for more suburban churches to meet the distinct movement of population from cities to suburban areas.[34] It was only a few years later that the Metuchen Church began its own major transformation into a suburban church. In the last year of Humphries' pastorate, Walter McHarg, who had directed the music of the church for ten years, resigned his post and Session hired J. F. Thomas as choir leader; in January 1942, Louise Halsey resigned as organist after 30 years, and William Silence was employed in her place.

In March 1942, Humphries reached 65 years of age, and some of the officers of the church felt that a change should be made. The pastor submitted a letter to Presbytery asking that the pastoral relation be dissolved as of September 1, 1942. A special congregation meeting, held at the close of service March 8, and presided over by Rev. Roland Bahnson of Grant Avenue Presbyterian Church, Plainfield, approved a resolution, by a vote of 64-47, that the congregation unite with the pastor in his request.[35] On March 15, Humphries notified the congregation by letter that his advancing years and declining energy were not sufficient to bring the growth that was necessary in a time of religious indifference. In April a pulpit committee was constituted under the chairmanship of Elder J. W. Clark. The committee visited the church in the neighboring community of Iselin, and their unanimous recommendation was approved by the congregation. On August 5 a call was extended to Rev. Adolph H. Behrenberg, pastor of the Presbyterian Church in Iselin, at a salary of $2600, use of the manse, and a month's annual vacation.[36] The next day Dr. Behrenberg accepted the call, saying that he was attracted by a church that could get along so well with its pastors, looking forward to the beginning of his service in September, and promising to his new congregation love, devotion and service.

In his 17 years as pastor, Rev. George Humphries had had to face problems that were unique and unprecedented in the entire history of the church in their effects upon human lives. He dealt with these challenges in the sure knowledge that the Christian command of love of fellow man gave him the tools to help raise men from despair and disillusionment. The judgment of his son is probably right, that "... he served his generation and his church well in one of the most difficult eras of our history."[37] With Humphries, too, ends the long history of this church as a small, essentially rural, self-contained congregation, whose continuity with its past was clearly visible over a period of more than 200 years. The mobility and the growth of the American population and the prosperity of its war and post-war decades, in short the tides of our contemporary world, were about to flood in to destroy the old and to permanently transform both the church and its community into something neither had ever been before — large, suburban, cosmopolitan.

CHAPTER XVI — FOOTNOTES

1. Biographical information is part of a letter written by Rev. Bertram Humphries, the pastor's son, February 1, 1967.
2. Session minutes, October 7, 1925, including a program of the service.
3. Session minutes, September 13, 1926.
4. For example, see Session minutes September 23, 1927; May 28, 1929.
5. Session minutes, April 7, July 2, October 1, 1929.
6. Session minutes, October 1, 1929.
7. Session minutes, January 16, 1938.
8. Session minutes, May 5, 1931; William H. Ayers, *A History of the First Presbyterian Church*, 1947, p. 31.
9. Minutes of congregation meeting, June 11, 1930.
10. Session minutes, October 15, 1930.
11. Session minutes, July 14, September 22, November 3, 1931, June 5, 1934.
12. Session minutes, January 8, 1935.
13. Minutes of Women's Guild, May 28, 1941.

14. Session minutes, June 4, 1941.

15. Letter of Rev. Bertram Humphries, February 1, 1967.

16. For instance, Session minutes, June 15, 1937.

17. *Metuchen, The Brainy Borough,* unpublished manuscript, ch. 4, pgs. 7-9.

18. Letter of Rev. Bertram Humphries, February 1, 1967.

19. *Ibid.*

20. *Ibid.*

21. Figures are taken from annual reports to the Presbytery contained in Session minutes.

22. Annual report of Guild for 1934-5.

23. Guild minutes, April 24, June 26, September 25, 1935, March 25, 1936.

24. Annual report of Guild for 1937-8.

25. Guild minutes, May 22, December 6, 1935.

26. Typewritten undated history of the Guild.

27. Minutes of Women's Missionary Society, October 4, 1940.

28. Minutes of Women's Missionary Society, October 3, 1941.

29. Annual meeting, Women's Missionary Society of Presbytery of Elizabeth, April 16, 1935. Mrs. J. W. Clark was an officer.

30. Program of ordination included in Session minutes.

31. Session minutes, October 22, 1940.

32. *Ibid.*

33. Session minutes, January 12, March 2, 1941.

34. Session minutes, November 4, 1941.

35. Minutes of congregation meeting, March 8, 1942.

36. Session minutes, April 12, 1942; minutes of congregation meeting, August 5, 1942.

37. Letter of Rev. Bertram Humphries, February 1, 1967.

Chapter XVII

ADOLPH BEHRENBERG – EXPANSION AND GROWTH — THE EMERGENCE OF A SUBURBAN CHURCH

"At a few moments before 12 ... O Holy Night will be sung, and then the bell will ring to call the faithful to prayers and the celebration of Holy Communion at the time of the Birthday of the King."

Parish News, December 15, 1948

"... you have a record of growth in your church that cannot be matched by any other church that I know of in the Synod."
Dr. Frank Getty, executive secretary, Synod of New Jersey, in Parish News, March 22, 1950

	Membership at End of Year	Number Received During Year
1946--------------------------------	755	102
1947--------------------------------	845	87
1948--------------------------------	962	165
1949--------------------------------	1050	130
1950--------------------------------	1115	138
1951--------------------------------	1170	126
1952--------------------------------	1253	162
1953--------------------------------	1342	153
1954--------------------------------	1388	157
1955--------------------------------	1488	191
1956--------------------------------	1603	226
1957--------------------------------	1712	203
1958--------------------------------	1788	187
1959--------------------------------	1902	211
1960--------------------------------	1983	235
1961--------------------------------	2078	238

THE TWENTY-FIVE YEARS, to the present, of the ministry of Dr. Behrenberg have witnessed the creation of a new church. The changes in this period have been revolutionary, and they have reflected the great economic and social transformation of New Jersey and the New York metropolitan area in the postwar period. Today the church not only serves vastly more people than ever before, but serves them in vastly different ways. But this growth and development did not come automatically. The changes that have transformed a small semi-rural community into a large suburban link in an urbanized and industrialized metropolitan area might simply have caused the church to atrophy and to cease being one of the primary religious and social servants of the community. That this did not happen, and that the church found the key to survival and prosperity was largely due to the leadership of its pastor in constantly urging his congregation to look ahead, and to realize that only by accommodating itself to swiftly changing needs could the church keep up with the present and continue to be of vital service to its larger community. The record shows, too, that the congregation was willing and able to follow this leadership.

It is not the intention of this chapter to record in full the history of its most recent quarter century. We stand too close to it to gain the advantage of perspective. To sketch the direction of growth, to indicate the proliferation of its services and activities, to record a few of the major developments will be sufficient to emphasize that in the post World War II era, the First Presbyterian Church of Metuchen became an institution that bore little resemblance to what it had been in the long years from James Pierson to George Humphries.

Adolph Behrenberg, ninth pastor of the church, graduated from the University of Pittsburgh in 1935, and two years later while a student at Princeton Theological Seminary accepted the opportunity to become a temporary supply preacher at the Presbyterian Church in Iselin.[1] A year later, on May 17, 1938, Reverend Behrenberg was ordained in the Iselin congregation by the Presbytery of Elizabeth. During the next four years he carried the heavy load of ministering to a congregation seriously affected by the problems of the depression while at the same time carrying on graduate study. He first earned a Master of Theology degree at Princeton, then a Doctor of Theology degree at Union Seminary, taking advantage of the opportunity to study under the great teachers of each institution. In the spring of 1942 families from Metuchen came to hear him and in August a call was extended to accept the pulpit of the Metuchen church. His service began on September 17 and on October 2 the pastor was officially installed, with Reverend Henry Sloan Coffin, president of Union Seminary, as the preacher.[2] The questions to the pastor and to the people were asked by Reverend Chester Davis, pastor of Rahway First Church; the charge to the pastor given by Dean Edward Roberts of Princeton Seminary; the charge to the people by Reverend Herbert England, pastor of Roselle First Church and Stated Clerk of Elizabeth Presbytery.

In 1942 the church itself was still the clapboard frame building that had been erected more than 100 years earlier. Adjacent on the east side was the sexton's cottage; to the west was the old lecture hall and church school building, and the new brick educational building erected in Humphries' pastorate. The parsonage had a large west wing, which had earlier been used for a school, and a porch on the front and west sides, both of which were removed to restore the building to its original simple and beautiful architecture. Extensive interior repair was carried out before the pastor moved in in December.[3] Church membership in 1941 numbered 340, of which 110 members pledged financial support; the Sunday School had an enrollment of 252. Receipts for operation were just short of $8000, and for benevolence just short of $1500.[4] Besides the pastor, the church employed a sexton, an organist and a choir director.

Innovations began slowly during the war years. The first Christmas Eve midnight communion service was held December 24, 1942, with about 440 in attendance, and 25 new members being received; it soon became an established tradition and one of the most beautiful of the annual services.[5] The next spring the original Board of Deacons was changed to a Deaconess Board of nine members, and provision was made to increase Session to twelve members.[6] Already people were joining the church in larger than usual numbers, 81 during 1943 and 84 during 1944. By the end of 1944 membership stood at 598, already considerably larger than ever before in its history; the next year it reached 675, about double what it was only four years earlier.[7] The young people's communicants class accounted for a considerable part of this increase, numbering 15 in 1943, 17 in 1944 and 30 in 1945. But the church thus far was still its traditional self. At the annual congregation meeting of March 21, 1944,

194

the pastor made special mention of three women who had been members 60 years or more: Mrs. Luther Smith, Mrs. Anna Crowell, who was present at the occasion, and Miss Lillian Van Sicklen; seven others had been in the church 50 years.[8] One small project of remodeling took place in the spring of 1945 when one end of the old kitchen in the church was reconstructed to make a Board Room where official bodies could hold meetings.[9] This room, in the northeast corner of the church adjacent to the sanctuary, was used by Session before church services until the major reconstruction of the church in 1958.

By the end of the war it became apparent that the church would have to undertake a major expansion in its program and facilities if it was to continue to serve the growing needs of the community. As early as January, 1945 Session had received a report that more than fifty young people were meeting regularly on Sunday evenings at the Y.M.C.A., and about 100 young people had been present at the Watch Night Service on New Year's Eve.[10] In addition, attendance at church services was growing large enough to create more demand for additional facilities and programs. In May, 1945 the pastor met with the officers of the church to discuss the idea of building a parish social hall, to serve as a social center for the congregation.[11] Dr. Behrenberg pointed out that the project would be consistent with the old Protestant tradition of the church as a parish house while still looking forward to serve new needs of the present.[12] A committee under Sterling Mayo was formed to study the project and propose it to the congregation. On June 7, 1945, a special congregation meeting was held to discuss the entire plan; about 75 parishioners attended. The meeting was moderated by W. R. Hale, who said that the committee was thinking in terms of a brick building modeled somewhat after the Grange Hall in Dayton, N. J. Mr. Mayo discussed details, including suggestions for a large auditorium, a social-dining hall, and a large kitchen. The location of the building was expected to be in the orchard between the manse and the church, and the probable cost was about $30,000. Others spoke, and architect's plans to harmonize the building with the recently constructed educational building were displayed. After general discussion about possible alternatives and the wisdom of the contemplated action, a resolution was introduced that a finance committee and a building committee be appointed, and the congregation undertake to raise $30,000 over a three year period beginning in October. After further discussion the resolution was carried with only three opposing votes. Thomas Ainslie was made chairman of the finance committee and Sterling Mayo chairman of the building committee.

In the light of subsequent events and the great use to which the new building was put, this first step was probably the most important single decision made by the congregation in the postwar period. It made it possible for the church to expand its programs and to serve its parish in many new ways. Subsequent decisions to undertake major capital improvements followed almost as a matter of course. With the decision to raise the money to build a social center, the congregation decided in effect that the church was going to undertake in a major way to meet the new challenges of contemporary society. Most appropriately, it was called a forward movement.

As preparations were undertaken for this new center, other changes were taking place. In 1947 the church decided to engage the services of a student minister from the Seminary.[13] In the spring of that same year the congregation undertook a colonial restoration of the interior of the church, including changes in the pulpit and choir loft; in June, Mrs. William Iobst began her tenure as church organist.[14]

1948 was the first great postwar year. Session approved building plans for the social center in January, a mortgage was secured, contracts were let, and in May, on Pentecost Sunday, the cornerstone was laid.[15] Final plans called for an auditorium with a capacity of 325, a banquet hall seating 250, which was also to serve as the main recreation room, an office, a lounge, and a kitchen, all to be enclosed in brick colonial style.[16]

The construction was completed over the summer and the building opened in the fall. Dedication ceremonies were held on Sunday afternoon October 24, after which a reception committee, including Mr. and Mrs. W. C. Behrenberg, parents of the pastor, Mr. and Mrs. Otto Hansen, and Mr. and Mrs. John MacWilliam, welcomed everyone to an open house.[17] Special events and entertainment were held each evening during the following week, culminating with the Harvest Home Festival when dinner was served to 400 parishioners.[18] The pastor hoped that the social center would unite the people of the church and the community and serve as a place of social gathering for people of all ages.[19] A House Committee of two elders and two trustees was set up to control use of the building by non-parish organizations.[20] That people were attracted to it was already being demonstrated by the increase in church membership itself. During 1948, 165 new members were received, at communion services on Ash Wednesday, Maundy Thursday, Pentecost, World-Wide Communion Sunday, and Christmas Eve. This was the largest number of new members received in any year of the church's history, and was not to be surpassed until 1955 and later. By the end of 1948 the membership stood at 962.[21]

Early in the year Dr. Behrenberg had reported to Session on a proposal for a new weekly paper to be mailed to each member of the church, beginning in the fall.[22] Final plans were made, and on September 8, 1948 the first issue of Parish News was published. The purpose of Parish News was explained as an effort to reach the congregation with announcements of parish work and knowledge of church activities, information about the next Sunday's service, marriages, deaths and other personal notices.[23] Sketches of church buildings for the cover were prepared by Mrs. Arthur Johnson. Over the years the little paper was to explain Christian and Presbyterian doctrines and ceremonies, the need for pledging and financial support, and the activities and meetings of various organizations. It proved immediately successful in giving a feeling of unity and common interest to the entire church family. By the spring of 1949, Parish News was arriving each Thursday in nearly 600 homes.

The completion of the social center and the inauguration of Parish News provided both the means and the opportunity to begin in a meaningful way to expand the activities of the church. At the 1949 annual meeting Dr. Behrenberg proposed setting aside the second Friday of each month as Parish Night, to develop programs in which all members could participate. Subsequently a schedule was set up, beginning with the Parish Night in March sponsored by the 20-30 Club, presenting the play *Mama Had a Hunch.*[24] Later events that year were sponsored by the Missionary Society, the Evening Circle, and the Group.[25]

On Friday, January 7, the pastor invited Professor Edward Jurji of Princeton to speak to an adult group on the subject of comparative religion; this was the first of a series of monthly Friday night talks which eventually became the Adult Education series.[26] In addition to this program, Dr. Behrenberg gave a series of talks based on the book *You and Psychiatry,* which proved so popular that a regular time was set aside on Wednesday evenings after the Bible service to conduct informal discussion meetings on other topics. So began what was to become a regular Wednesday evening book discussion group.[27] In a different type of activity, a Saturday night Open House for high school students became an immediate success, with about 175 usually in attendance.[28]

In the spring of 1949, discussions were held concerning the organization of a daily Nursery School, to be sponsored by the Evening Circle, with professional teachers and the charging of tuition.[29] Under the guidance of Mrs. Robert Fleetham, equipment was bought, enrollment taken, teachers hired, and plans approved by the State supervising agency.[30] In September the school officially opened with eighteen children, and rapidly became well established as a valuable non-denominational service to the community at large.

The changes that came in 1948 and 1949 were so extensive, both in the range of services, facilities and activities offered, and in the number of people involved, that the church as an institution was from this time on permanently changed from what it had been. Church membership was not only growing but was constantly changing as well, as people moved away or left the community. Over 300 members left the church in the five years between 1948 and the end of 1952; yet the net gain in membership in that time was about 400. Thus the church was constantly being renewed, and its older families represented a much smaller percentage of the total membership. While the larger membership brought in representatives of many nationalities,[31] it was still true nevertheless that the economic status of its members did not vary appreciably. By the end of 1950, Dr. Behrenberg had received more members in eight years than James Mason in his entire span of almost half a century; by the spring of 1951, more than 1000 persons had joined the church in the present pastorate.[32]

New organizations and new programs continued to make their appearance. In the fall of 1950 the traditional mid-week service held in the Educational Building was changed into a Bible Study Hour and moved to the lounge of the social center. Hymns and scripture readings were omitted and a more informal atmosphere established in an effort to attract more people to this serious study.[33] A new women's Service Circle, sponsored by the Guild, was formed in January, 1952, and the next month the Couples' Club, succeeding the organization called the Group, held its initial meeting.[34] During this same year the church helped to initiate and contributed financially to the project which resulted in the founding of the Community Presbyterian Church of Edison. Its organization meeting on Sunday, November 16, 1952, was, most appropriately, presided over by Dr. Behrenberg, who was serving that year as moderator of the Presbytery of Elizabeth.[35]

After the building of the social center, the next major improvement in the church was the installation of a new organ, to replace one dating back to 1905. Collection of money had begun as early as 1952, and in the spring of 1954 fund raising began in earnest. A committee under William

Silence as chairman and Albert Bradshaw as treasurer organized a canvass of the parish in April and May to solicit pledges toward the goal of $55,000.[36] Within a month over $20,000 was raised in pledges from individual families and from organizations in the church; in the fall the order was placed with the Austin Corporation of Hartford, Conn., with installation planned for the summer of 1955.[37] The instrument is a three-manual organ, with 1745 pipes, including two electronic 32´ pedal stops. On Sunday, October 30, 1955, the new organ and chimes were dedicated at the morning services, and in the afternoon an impressive dedicatory recital was performed by Dr. Charlotte Garden, playing both classical and contemporary organ music.[38]

In 1953 it became apparent that the duties of the pastor would have to be shared with an associate minister. In November of that year Session decided to ask Reverend Benjamin Whitaker, who had been assisting in the church since 1949, to accept a call to the new position. The responsibilities of the job were worked out in detail and reviewed with Reverend Whitaker by a Session committee. They included mainly responsibility for youth work, released time, regular parish calling, and general assistance to the minister.[39] The congregation accepted the recommendation of Session in January, 1954, and on February 21, Reverend Whitaker was officially installed as associate pastor.[40]

Growth and change came at an accelerated pace in the last half of the 1950s. The way had been prepared by the decision made in the fall of 1954 to start double sessions of both church and Sunday School in September, 1955.[41] In further planning for this change, Session decided to hold communion on the first Sunday of each month at 9:30 A.M.[42] Other changes included the assignment of the associate pastor to the confirmation class, and the hiring of a part-time director of religious education.[43] The double sessions proved immediately popular and undoubtedly helped to make 1956 the year of greatest growth yet, with 226 new members added and total membership passing 1600.[44] Not until the 1960s did more join in a single year. The Sunday School of course shared in this increase. Especially since 1952 the number of children enrolled in Sunday School accelerated at an increasing rate and by 1956 the total number of teachers and students was reaching close to 1000. Before long other services were added to accommodate more people, a 7:30 Christmas Eve service in 1957, an 8 A.M. Easter service in 1958 and a Good Friday service in 1959. Finally, in this growth year of 1956, a new west wing was added to the social center to provide additional office space and meeting rooms.[45] Improved financial capability supported expanding budgets, and when the benevolence budget for 1957 was established, it included for the first time support for the United Mission Hospital in Nepal.[46]

This great decade of dramatic growth was climaxed by the largest single undertaking in the history of the church, the forward movement of 1958. It was first planned for at the Joint Board Dinner meeting of February 5, 1957. At that meeting Dr. Behrenberg emphasized the overcrowded conditions of the Sunday School and the imperative need to expand its facilities. Since 1947 Sunday School enrollment had almost quadrupled in ten years, and the added capacity of the social center and double sessions were simply inadequate to meet the need. It had also become apparent by this time that the original siding on the old frame church needed a major rehabilitation if it was to survive as a building. It was proposed that the exterior of the church be resurfaced in brick, and a new bell tower and steeple added in front.[47] The new plans were approved for submission to the congregation, with Thomas Ainslie as general chairman, Miles Oppenheim and Ralph Preston as co-chairmen of the finance committee, and Saxon Palmeter and Reuben Hager as co-chairmen of the building committee. After congregational approval was given unanimously at the annual meeting, the services of a professional fund raiser were engaged and a goal of $250,000 set,[48] an amount which was three times as large as the total receipts for all purposes in 1957. The final plans provided for eight new classrooms and three large auditoria for the Sunday School as well as other needed improvements in the educational building; exterior reconstruction of the church and the addition of choir rooms, cloak rooms and a session room; and the building of a new chapel.

The energies of the entire congregation were mobilized and supreme efforts made by all organizations of the church and by individual families in the sacrificial giving needed to reach the goal. The entire project moved forward with great success. The ground breaking was held in a snowstorm after church on Sunday, February 16, 1958, with the four co-chairmen of the building and finance committees taking part. In April Session decided to move all church services to the Forum Theater on Main Street until construction work was finished.[49] Services in the theater continued until Sunday, October 5 when the cornerstone, containing historic documents, was laid. Finally on Sunday, December 14 the entire project was complete and dedication ceremonies were held for the new Sunday School addition, the new chapel, and the rebuilt church.[50] The creation of the present church was at last complete, an event which may appropriately mark the conclusion of this history.

The events of the decade between 1948 and 1958 had equipped the church to provide a broad range of services and activities to its congregation and to the community. Consistent with this constant outreach, Dr. Behrenberg emphasized in his sermons the responsibility of the Christian to relate his religious beliefs and attitudes to the issues and problems faced by the nation and the outside world. To renew his own understanding and to bring his views through the Christian ministry to his congregation, the pastor began in 1947 to make summer trips to various countries, and to relate his experiences in a series of fall lectures. These trips have now taken him to 105 countries and seven times around the world, and he has had opportunities to meet both humble citizens and important leaders, both lay and religious, of many lands. Combining the roles of scholarly investigator, art collector, and vacationing traveler, Dr. Behrenberg has demonstrated by example that the practicing Christian cannot stand aloof from his society or from his world, and that Protestant Christianity has much to contribute to the discussion of the great social, economic and political problems of the modern day. Though he ministers to a vastly larger and more mobile congregation, the pastor in this commitment stands in the great tradition of James Pierson, Azel Roe, James Mason and George Humphries. Each in his own time, and according to his own lights, emphasized, in the words of Gilbert Tennent, that "we were born not merely for ourselves, but the Publick Good, which as members of society we are obliged ... to promote."

In America 250 years is a long time. In this one church over that time thousands of individuals, through voluntary association, have committed a significant part of the effort and direction of their individual lives. Though the farmers of the early congregation are no longer present, over the years the members of the church have come from many different backgrounds and have joined for many different reasons. What is the tie that binds them together? Of what does its unity and its creative vigor consist? An incident occurred one Easter dawn in the early 1950s when a few members of Session were gathered in the Board Room at the northeast corner of the church just before sunrise service. It was a clear morning and as the outside light became brighter, the rays of the rising sun suddenly stabbed through the tree branches into the east window and filled the room with sunlight. The men watched silently for a minute or so; then one said simply, "Christ is risen." In that faith has lived and prospered the First Presbyterian Church of Metuchen.

CHAPTER XVII — FOOTNOTES

1. Biographical information is taken from a letter by Dr. Behrenberg to the writer, May 2, 1966.
2. Session minutes, October 2, 1942; Annual Report of the Pastor, 1966. President Coffin had recently conferred the degree of Doctor of Theology on Dr. Behrenberg.
3. Letter by Dr. Behrenberg, May 2, 1966; Annual Report of the Pastor, 1966; newspaper article by Kay Rodney.
4. Session minutes, March 2, 1941.
5. Session minutes, December 24, 1942.
6. Session minutes, March 2, 1943; Congregational Meeting, March 16, 1943.
7. Congregational Meeting, March 20, 1945; March 19, 1946.
8. The seven were Mrs. Grace Rule, Mrs. Charles Veghte, Mr. and Mrs. William H. Ayers, Mrs. Ambrose Mundy, Mrs. Anita Bloomfield, and Mrs. W. T. Campbell.
9. Session minutes, February 25, March 29, 1945.
10. Session minutes, January 2, 1945.
11. Information in this paragraph is taken from minutes of the Congregational Meeting of June 7, 1945.
12. Letter by Dr. Behrenberg, May 2, 1966.
13. Joint Board Dinner Meeting, January 21, 1947.
14. Congregational Meeting, April 13, 27, 1947; Session minutes, June 3, 1947.
15. Session minutes, January 6, February 1, May 16, 1948; Congregational Meeting, January 20, 1948.
16. Dedication Souvenir Program of the Presbyterian Social Center.
17. Mr. Hansen was general contractor, and Mr. MacWilliam the architect.
18. Session minutes, October 20, 1948; Parish News, October 6, November 10, 1948.
19. Parish News, October 20, 1948.
20. Parish News, November 3, 1948.
21. Congregational Meeting, January 18, 1949.
22. Session minutes, April 6, 1948.
23. Parish News, September 8, 1948.

24. Congregational Meeting, January 18, 1949; Session minutes, February 1, 1949; Parish News, January 27, 1949.
25. Parish News, January 6, February 9, 1949.
26. Parish News, December 30, 1948.
27. Parish News, January 6, March 2, 1949.
28. Parish News, February 3, 1949.
29. Session minutes, March 1, 1949; Parish News, March 9, 1949.
30. Parish News, May 18, 1949.
31. The writer recalls recent years when the tenor section of the Adult Choir included Robert Celentano, John Kostopolous, Douglas Reisinger, Victor Chu, and William Iobst.
32. Parish News, March 28, 1951.
33. Parish News, September 13, October 4, 1950.
34. Parish News, January 23, 30, February 6, 13, 1952.
35. Parish News, February 13, April 16, May 6, November 12, 1952; letter by Dr. Behrenberg, May 2, 1966; a program of the service is included in Session minutes.
36. Session minutes, February 2, March 2, 1954; Parish News, May 12, 1954.
37. Session minutes, June 1, September 7, 1954; Parish News, May 26, June 2, 1954.
38. Program of Service of Dedication of New Organ and Chimes and Dedicatory Recital, October 30, 1955.
39. Session minutes, November 3, December 1, 1953. William H. Ayers and Edwin Risler constituted the committee.
40. Congregational Meeting, January 26, 1954; program of installation, February 21, 1954.
41. Session minutes, October 5, 1954.
42. Session minutes, March 1, 1955. Communion is now served twenty times a year.
43. Session minutes, October 5, 1954; October 4, 1955.
44. Congregational Meeting, January 22, 1957.
45. Joint Board Dinner meeting, February 7, 1956; Session minutes, September 4, 1956.

46. Session minutes, October 2, 1956.
47. Joint Board Dinner meeting, February 5, 1957; brochure on the Forward Movement.
48. Congregational Meeting, February 24, 1957.
49. Session minutes, April 19, 1958.
50. Session minutes, September 21, October 7, 1958.

Chapter XVIII

THE PRESENT CHURCH IN ITS WORLD

"We are too often a church family not because of what we share in Christ but because of what we share in the world. Take almost any local Protestant church and you will discover that it cuts a thin, exclusive strip through the social order: the people will belong mostly to one political party, one race and one ethnic group. They will stand generally on the same academic, cultural and economic plane. These similarities are often wholesome ties but they are not the bond of Christian unity."
– Sermon by Dr. Kyle Haselden, December 12, 1965,
at Grosse Point Memorial Church,
Grosse Point Farms, Michigan

"I remember most the rally at the Presbyterian Church in Metuchen. I enjoyed myself there more than anywhere else. I had never spoken to a large crowd of white people before.... A lot of people told me afterwards how well I had done."
– Ben Cheney, 12 years old, Meridian, Mississippi

"I remember the nice people there ... and the most important thing — the night we spoke at the Metuchen church and gave our opinions about Mississippi."
– Pat James, 13 years old, Meridian, Mississippi
(As quoted in Sunday Home News, February 28, 1965.
The evening referred to was Sunday, August 30, 1964)

IT SEEMS FITTING, as a conclusion to this history, to relate in some detail the range of activity that engage the energies of the church today. A review of the year from Advent 1964 to Advent 1965 will serve very well in giving this chronology of the present.[1] The membership was at its peak — 2289 at the end of 1964, 2321 a year later. The congregation supported an operating budget of over $96,000 in 1965, and a benevolence budget of over $31,000.

Advent, the prophesy and fulfillment of Christ's birth, began Sunday, November 29, 1964 with the traditional processional hymn, O Come, O Come Emmanuel. The advent sermon titles that year were: God so Loved the World; Hail Mary, Full of Grace; My Soul Doth Magnify; Peace on Earth. On each of the four Sundays an additional advent candle was lit. Special music was presented by the younger choirs on December 13, entitled God's Son is Born, and a week later the Senior Choir sang Von Hulse's Christmas Oratorio.

The 20-30 and Concord Clubs, through the Adult Education Committee, sponsored two lectures by Dr. Robert K. Alsofrom on December 6 and January 8: Growing Up in the Modern World, and Major Causes of Divorce in American Life. These two clubs also sponsored a Christmas dance on Parish Night. On December 18 the Couples' Club heard assistant minister Mr. George Thomas give an illustrated lecture on the Holy Land. One of the great family days of fellowship, the annual Holly Fair, was held on December 4.

The Women's Supplement to the Parish News recorded the historic work of existing women's groups in uniting to form one organization for women's work in the church. Recommendations of the denomination were being followed in this work; at the same time some of the valuable aspects of the earlier organization, such as the Service and Fellowship Circles, were being retained. During the month of December Mr. and Mrs. Miklos Komoroczy, who had come from Hungary after the revolution of 1956, became citizens of the United States; Mr. William Silence completed ten years as Clerk of the Session.

Neighborhood caroling was carried on by youth groups on Sunday the 20th, and by 20-30 and Concord Clubs on the 21st. On Christmas Eve family services were held at 5 and 7:30 P.M., with the Carol Choir and Boys' Choir participating in the first, and the Junior and Youth Choirs in the second. The Westminster Choir led the 10 P.M. Communion Service, first instituted in 1962. This was followed by the impressive and beautiful midnight service, heralded by the ringing of the church bell and the singing of O Holy Night, on this occasion by George Hunter, and ending with the friendly greeting of Merry Christmas. It was estimated that the twelve services between December 13 and 27 were attended by almost 5000 people. Parish News of December 24 carried Christmas greetings to the congregation, signed by the pastor.

In January, with resumption of normal schedules, Contemporary Books Group devoted its Wednesday evening meeting to a discussion of the book *Feminine Mystique.* The three Youth Fellowships resumed their winter programs. The congregation was reminded that the pastor was in his study each morning from 8 to 1, and that Reverend George Chorba, the associate pastor was in his office Tuesday through Friday mornings.

On Mission Sunday, January 10, the sermon was preached by Reverend Gladstone Ntlabati, ordained minister of the Methodist Church of South Africa. Reverend Ntlabati, studying for his doctorate at Yale Divinity School, is one of the leaders in the struggle for freedom of non-whites in South Africa. At the Sunday evening chapel service on January 17 the speaker was Reverend J. Metz Rollins, Associate Executive Director of the Commission on Religion and Race of the Presbyterian Church. The quarterly meeting of the Men's Club heard a talk by County Superintendent of Schools Dr. Robert Blunt.

The annual congregation meeting, at which reports by officers and boards were presented, was held on Tuesday, January 26. Nine elders, four deaconesses, four trustees, four members of the Board of Christian Education, and twelve members for the new Board of Deacons were elected at the meeting. The Board of Deacons inaugurated the new Shepherd program in an effort to involve more people in the activities of the church. On the 27th the formal reorganization of women's groups took place with the inauguration of Mrs. Alfred Urffer as the first president of the new Women's Association. The Joint Board dinner, to make plans for the ensuing year, was held on February 2. In connection with these events, it was reported that in 1965 Mr. Elliott Mayo was in his 10th Anniversary Year as superintendent of the Sunday School; a similar milestone was being observed by Mrs. Richard Condon as Director of Christian Education, and Mrs. Thomas Peake as finance officer. The pastor reported that he was now the second oldest in point of service of active ministers in the Elizabeth Presbytery.

In February, a contribution of $8000 to the building fund of the Oak Tree Presbyterian Church was acknowledged by Dr. Chester Davis, the organizing pastor. His letter of gratitude stated, "Without this and the previous help your church has shown and your continued interest it would seem impossible to establish a church here...." It is indeed fitting that a history that began with the establishment of the Woodbridge Church by parishioners from Newbury, and that eventually led to the founding of the Metuchen church by parishioners from Woodbridge, should come now, after 250 years, to the record of the efforts made by parishioners from Metuchen to help establish in 1952 the Edison Church and in 1965 the church at Oak Tree.

The congregation was reminded in February that the pastor called on members who were sick or hospitalized and on prospective new members. Regular calling was divided between Reverend Chorba and Mr. Thomas. The social center was busy with parent-son dinners for seven scout troops; all together twelve such groups hold meetings in church buildings.

Lent began on Ash Wednesday, March 3, with titles of Lenten sermons given in advance. Over the course of the year there were sermons on doctrine, on Christian practice, and on the relationship of the church to the world and national community. The pastor explained the nature of his Lenten sermons as discussing how the Christian can live effectively in a world of diverse opinions.

The fourth annual Lenten School began on March 10. Two evening courses were held, one entitled This I Believe: Protestant Affirmations for Today, conducted by Dr. Cyrus Pangborn, Professor of Religion at Douglass College; and one on the Household of Faith and The Household of God, conducted by Reverend Chorba. Young people of the church were offered three elective courses during Lent: Contemporary Judaism; The Language of Christian Faith; The Mission of the Church in New Nations.

A class of 70 eighth-graders had been studying since September to prepare themselves for confirmation and admission to the church as adult members. They were to be examined publicly before Session on the Saturday before Palm Sunday. During March, high school fellowship groups were meeting to consider carrying out a summer mission project in Wilmington, Delaware.

Special events marked the approach to Holy Week. On Passion Sunday, April 4, about 175 choristers took part in the Sixth Annual Hymn Festival. On Palm Sunday the Senior Choir presented Mendelssohn's Elijah to inaugurate the commemoration of Jesus' last week of life. On April 15, "the bells will ring tonight, on Maundy Thursday, to remind the people of the Faith that this was the night on which Jesus was betrayed...." Communion services were held on the evening of Maundy Thursday and Good Friday, with confirmation of the young people who had completed their training at each of the services.

The joy of the resurrection was marked first by sunrise communion service at six o'clock on Easter morning, when the rays of the early sun came streaming horizontally into the church. Later services were held at 8, 9:30 and 11, with choirs and trumpeters singing out the tune, Jesus

211

Christ is Risen Today. It was later estimated that over 2000 people had attended the four Easter services, and about 4500 the nine services during Holy Week.

At the end of April the church membership was reported at 2344. It was expected that the Oak Tree Church, to which Metuchen had thus far donated $15,000 would be officially incorporated by the Presbytery in 1965. In May, Reverend Robert Seaman of Chester, Pa. became the regular pastor of that church.

The month of May brought a variety of speakers. Richard Johnson, Deputy Director of the Kilmer Job Corps Center, came to discuss the activities of the Center; Donald Herzberg, executive director of the Eagleton Institute at Rutgers, spoke to the Men's Club; Morris Milgram gave a talk on New Frontiers in Housing. Both Mr. Johnson and Mr. Milgram were sponsored by the Church and Society Committee.

In other activities, the Board of Trustees purchased a residence on Laureldale Avenue to house the sexton and his family, before demolition of the old house adjacent to the church. Young people attended a Youth Weekend at the Presbyterian Camp at Island Heights. The Contemporary Books Group met to select their books for the following year's study. The Couples Club invited the New Hope Baptist Choir to give a concert. Mr. Richard Killmer became the new student assistant minister, replacing Mr. Thomas, and Mr. Channing Coppage was employed as director of the senior choir. On May 23, the church organist Gretchen Iobst and alto Beverly Hensler, presented An Hour of Music.

On Sunday, May 30, Dr. Bethel Fleming of United Mission Hospital spoke. The coffee hour for her after the service was also a farewell to Mr. Thomas. The Senior Choir held its annual dinner at the Brunswick Inn. The second Sunday of June was Children's Day, with the sacrament of baptism and the promise of the parents to raise their child in the Christian faith. Parish News of June 17 carried statistics of the denomination reported by the General Assembly. The United Presbyterian Church had well over three million members and total receipts of over $305,000,000. The per capita giving to all causes of $90.55 was third largest among all denominations. Of the five largest congregations in the nation the only one east of the Mississippi was First Church of Westfield, with 4545 listed members.

Mr. Killmer assisted for the first time with church services on June 13, and on the following Sunday a dedication service was held for the fifteen young people and five adults comprising the mission team going to Wilmington, Delaware under the direction of Reverend Chorba. A farewell coffee for the pastor was held on June 27 just prior to his leaving on his 19th annual summer journey and his seventh trip around the world.

In July and August one service only, at 9:30, was held each Sunday, with Reverend Chorba and Mr. Killmer sharing the preaching duties. Daily Vacation Bible School, held July 12 to 23 on the theme God and His World, enrolled 96 children from the various churches taking part. Youth Fellowship activities included a Sandy Hook Beach Party, bicycle trips to County parks, a trip to art museums in New York, and a variety of activity in drama, book discussion, and hootenanny. Nearly 180 young people participated in some phase of these activities.

Church service on July 11 was conducted by members of the mission team who had spent a week at the First and Olivet Presbyterian Church in Wilmington, an inner-city church, aiding in painting and redecorating the interior of the old church in an atmosphere of Christian fellowship. Nine young people shared the responsibilities of the service, with the sermon entitled Youth in Mission. On July 18 nine families were hosts to visitors from the Kilmer Job Corps Center on a day when rain forced an indoor program. A successful cookout was held early in August. The Senior High Fellowship acted as hosts to the Corpus Christi Youth Choir, stopping by on August 1 for a picnic and concert in the course of their national tour. The sermon by Mr. Killmer on August 25 was entitled Freedom Now, a service in which the Call to Worship repeated the words of the freedom song, "How many roads must a man walk down before people call him a man...."

The summer months brought letters from Dr. Behrenberg, which were mimeographed in the church office and distributed on Sundays to the congregation. His annual midsummer letter was written from Katmandu, where since 1957 the Metuchen church has provided the rent for Surendra Bhawan, a 65-room former palace used by the United Mission Hospital. Three successive sermons by Mr. Killmer were entitle Love of Self; Love of God; Love of Others.

Autumn began on September 12 with the pastor's annual sermon on Religious and Allied Observations Following a Trip Around the World. Six Monday evening lectures at the Social Center, plus one with colored slides, recounted the trip in detail, with the free will offering going to support the 250th Anniversary Fund of the Church. Choirs, fellowships, boards and clubs resumed normal activities; so also for Sunday School and church services. The two adult Bible classes, one on Tuesday morning conducted by Reverend Chorba, and one on Wednesday evening by Dr. Behrenberg, were resumed. The Sunday School used the Christian Faith and Life Curriculum; by October the released time program for grades 1-6 on Friday afternoons was again under way. Bibles were presented to 4th graders on the last Sunday in September. About 175 adults were needed to carry on the Sunday School and released time programs, a major educational enterprise. Nursery School resumed with an enrollment of 60 children, including representatives of Jewish, Catholic and other Protestant denominations as well as Presbyterian.

In the early fall, Parish News reported the death of Hugh Farrell, 15 years an elder, 10 years as Sunday School superintendent, 30 years a member of the church. Youth fellowships went on their annual Fall Retreat. 20-30 Club brought a speaker on Rossmoor's Leisure World. Dr. Behrenberg wore a brilliant new robe in the colors of doctor of theology from Union Seminary. Several church groups participated in the Metuchen

Country Fair on Saturday, October 2. The next day was World Wide Communion Sunday.

The first of three Parish Night Family Dinners, replacing the old Harvest Home Festival, was held on October 8 with about 175 attending. Reverend Norman Koehler of the Board of Ecumenical Missions, spoke on the world mission of the church. October was an important month financially, as the Budget Committee under direction of the Board of Trustees put together the proposed budget for the next year, and the Stewardship Committee sent out letters and pledge cards to the congregation explaining the financial needs of the church and emphasizing the Christian responsibility of stewardship.

A portrait of Dr. Behrenberg, painted by Mrs. Arthur Johnson, former president of the Women's Guild, was presented to the church by the artist and hung in the Session room with the portraits of other ministers of the church. An appeal for volunteer therapists for continuing exercise treatment of one of the children of the congregation received an overwhelming response from the people.

The Women's Association held a workshop for all activities circles, including Service, Garden, Tally Group, Fellowship, and Sewing. Six Study Circles were also active. Plans were made for a Rummage Sale, a visit to Roosevelt Hospital, and a Rally Day luncheon. A luncheon meeting of the Association heard a talk by a Radcliffe professor of dramatics and literature.

A college night was held on Sunday evening the 31st, with admissions directors or representatives of many Presbyterian colleges present to consult with prospective students. That day was Reformation Sunday, and the morning service honored Martin Luther with a singing of A Mighty Fortress is Our God. The sermon was entitled The Saints Come Marching.

November 7 was Commitment Sunday when the congregation returned their pledge cards to support the proposed budget, and a Litany of Dedication was read at the service. Members not returning pledge cards were subsequently contacted by a member of the visitation committee.

Benevolent giving, now known as General Mission to distinguish it from the needs of the local church, was channeled through four main boards of the denomination. These are the Commission on Ecumenical Missions and Relations, the Board of National Missions, the Board of Christian Education, and the Board of Pensions. Other money went to such groups as the World and National Councils of Churches and the American Bible Society.

The All-Church Nominating Committee met on Sunday the 14th to prepare a list of candidates for positions on the various boards, to be elected at the annual meeting in January. The completion of the church school library and the purchase of some adult reference books were made possible by generous gifts from individual church members. The 20-30 Club heard Mr. Samuel Tate on Witchcraft as a Religion. The Church and Society Committee sought host families for Job Corps guests at Thanksgiving dinner. The death of Harry L. Vincent, clerk of the Session for 25 years, was noted in Parish News.

Young people signed up for fall elective courses running over a period of five weeks: The Church, Race and Poverty; Psychology and Christianity; The First Century Church; The Last Temptation of Christ. The Senior High group attended a performance of Sodom and Gomorrah in New York; at Thanksgiving time they paid a visit to the Middlesex Nursing Home. The Middlers enjoyed a hayride and the Junior Highs held a discussion on civil rights.

On Thanksgiving Sunday the processional hymn was Now Thank We All Our God. The stewardship campaign was completed, and on November 30 plans were to be revealed concerning the new capital campaign of the United Presbyterian denomination. Thanksgiving Eve service, sponsored by the Metuchen-Edison Council of Churches, was held in First Church at 8 P.M., with Reverend Chorba officiating, and Reverend Joseph Dale of New Hope Baptist, Reverend Hugh Fryer of St. Luke's Episcopal, and Reverend Gary Looman of the Reformed Church taking part in the service. The next Sunday was the first Sunday of Advent.

CHAPTER XVIII — FOOTNOTES

1. All of the material in this chapter is taken from Parish News, church programs, and annual reports.